EQUANIMITY

THE DIARY OF A CEO IN CRISIS

Simon Leslie

D1160793

Copyright © 2022 All rights reserved.

ISBN: 9781916105133

No part of this book may be used or reproduced in any manner whatsoever without written permission from the author. Brief passages may be quoted for the purposes of interviews, reviews, or press with permission and must be credited.

Every effort has been made to ensure this book is free from errors or omissions. However, the publisher, the author, the editor or their respective employees or agents, shall not accept responsibility for injury, loss, or damage occasioned to any person acting or refraining from action as a result of material in this book, whether or not such injury, loss, or damage in any way due to any negligent act or omission, breach of duty, or default on the part of the publisher, the author, the editor or their respective employees or agents.

Publisher: Lucky Leslie Publishing

Cover design by: Agus Budiyono
Edited by Kirsten Rees | Book Editor & Author Coach
Interviews edited by Gerry Ricketts

Connect with the author: Instagram: @simon_leslie21
www.luckyleslie.com

ACKNOWLEDGMENTS

Thank you Nats, Benjy, Zac, Scott, George,
and Bolt for being great support during this time.

Woody, I appreciate the constant belief
and inspiration.

Robin for always fighting to the very end
no matter what.

And to Jim and Michael for putting up with me.

I'M A STORYTELLER and this is a real story. I am struggling to believe it's even true. It's still really hard to believe the world went this mad for so long. The pages in this book contain the thoughts and feelings of my adventures in 2020/1. How I felt, how I behaved, and what I did to rebuild a devastated business. It's what I did to stay sane, together with a collection of stories from the forty-plus people who helped me keep my ship afloat. And how the messages will help you through whatever you need to fix.

Anyone who thinks they don't want problems, is not living to their potential. Everyone needs a good set of problems to grow.

The people in this book unintentionally became my support and beacons of light. They probably don't even realize how much they helped me, how some of their messages gave me inspiration when I needed it. I am sure they will inspire you when you need it too.

This is advice from some of the best people I've had conversations with and the lessons I'm now able to share with you after coming out thriving. It's an account of how they helped me, inspired my teams, and made us think about how to survive the worst event our company and sector had ever seen.

They shared ideas, inspiration, motivation, wisdom, thinking, and so much kindness. If you pay close attention, you too will find the answers. No matter what battle you face, this book will be full to the brim with ideas on how to overcome them.

The pandemic allowed me to tell my story, to share who I am, how strong I found out I was. I was uncomfortable, I was scared, I was lost. I was also determined, I believed, I remained disciplined and was full of faith. And so, with hindsight, it became the best thing that ever happened to me.

As a result of this experience, I will make myself available to anyone who needs help, wherever they are in the world. If you have a problem, and no one else can help, reach out and I will do my best to support you. The past couple of years have definitely improved all my skills: from negotiating, selling, doing big and mega deals, stress management, managing people and difficult situations, cash management and finding a way where one does not seem to exist.

CONTENTS

EQUANIMITY THE DIARY OF A CEO IN CRISIS

1

NO ONE KNOWS HOW TOUGH YOU ARE, UNTIL BEING TOUGH IS THE ONLY OPTION

IMAGINE A THOUSAND-PIECE PUZZLE in the wrong box. It's not impossible to do, but it's a lot tougher than it needs to be. At the end of February 2020 my puzzle was coming together, with about 250 pieces left to finish off my twenty-five years of business. Then without notice, along comes this virus, and in a second, my pieces are all over the floor. Many of the pieces disappeared and some broke, so putting this jigsaw puzzle back together was going to be even more challenging than I thought. Some might say 'why bother?' and 'just get a new puzzle'.

I started this book with the word 'imagine', and in the last couple of years I have had to have a very creative imagination. The words to the John Lennon song gave me hope, gave me belief. I needed all my self-courage and self-determination, as well as help from a lot of friends. Some started out as friends, others became friends along the way. My courage came from a place of not letting people down, being a giver and pleaser – some of which was seriously tested during this period.

I was also surprised by how people behaved, not towards me, but in general with each other. While some showed great courage, others were selfishly courageous. This was a new term for greedy swines. We all had to live with less, we were spending less, we all had more time than we knew what to do with and that was unsettling. This crisis revealed people's true characters.

2020 turned out to be a year of not enough. I don't have enough to survive, I'm not healthy enough, not loved enough, not cared for enough, not thin enough, and the one I heard the most I'm not good enough. It wasn't a year to get what you wanted; it was a year we really needed to appreciate what we had. The lack of gratitude is what held so many back during it all.

This book is the story of how I went about putting our business back together, using insights and stories from around the world. It is the combination of these messages, how we all got through 2020/1 and how in December we were back in the black, despite the worst market for travel and its media we had ever seen.

This was worse than all the events that had plagued the travel industry. From 9/11, through the financial crises and every other challenge of the 21st century combined. Our airline clients lost over a hundred billion dollars in 2020.

We went into 2020 as the biggest publisher in the world of inflight magazines, we had a content studio and a fledgling television business. Our nearest competitor had four magazines, we had thirty-six. We produced amazing content and sold advertising against it in London, Singapore, and Miami working with the biggest travel brands on the planet.

I gave the governments a regular kicking for their inaction and decision-making, yet I did not envy the job they had to do. We stopped behaving using common sense, and moved to scientists running the show, that was quite scary. The thing is this, common sense ain't that common anymore. This book will give you the strength to deal with whatever life throws at you. It doesn't matter if you are in business or work for someone else, the secrets that it shares will turn you into a better human being, it did me. It helped me make sense of the 'non-sense', it helped articulate exactly what my message was, and how I could use it to help so many more people. The playbook I used was taking the best bits from all of the messages we received.

2020 was a time we blamed fear, anxiety, stress, and our wellbeing on the virus. In previous years we blamed the same conditions on our bosses, parents, friends, or partners. It's always somebody else's fault. Remember, the only person holding you back is the person in the mirror. That person will fill you with enough great stories to fill a book much bigger than this one.

I always say that when you point one finger at someone else, three fingers are still pointing back at you. In every situation before you blame anyone else, ask yourself the three most important questions:

1) What did I learn from this?
2) What was good about this?
3) What could I do differently next time?

2

LIVING
A GREAT LIFE

FEBRUARY 2020

THIS WAS GOING TO BE A GREAT YEAR, an election year, a year filled with optimism. The company had just recorded its best-ever year. We had just delivered 25% bottom line growth, now that's not bad for a company entering its twenty-sixth year on the planet. I had booked a ton of trips; my wife was turning fifty and I wanted to spoil her. She had pretty high expectations, since on my fiftieth I went off to the World Cup finals in Moscow with my friends.

As we lay by the pool on a private island in the Seychelles, Gregory, our butler, brought us breakfast. I turned to her and said this was going to be a special year for all of us.

Some might say 'how wrong you were'. And I would argue, 'this has been one of the greatest times of our lives'. While it clearly hasn't gone to plan, I think my family, my teams and myself have learned so much about ourselves and are now more aware as humans. We all had to take a deep, hard look inside, we had to hold up the mirror and decide who we wanted to be at the end of this. I finally got what I had always been craving, TIME. The sad thing was watching so many people waste that opportunity by being scared, by worrying and not using it as the reset it had become. Most people fell into two camps: worriers or deniers.

Time is the only commodity we are not getting any more of, it's precious and valuable. So many wasted and abused it. Every day is a miracle, and too many let it pass without fully living and being present. Our biggest mistake is that too many of us live on autopilot. That's not living at all.

Every day is a gift, we should appreciate our time and who we are spending it with. Also, consider how we look after ourselves, our families, those we are in business with, and the people who make our lives what they should be. This was a time to decide who we wanted to be, what we wanted to do and what perfection could look and feel like.

It's about understanding our own power and energy source.

'An energy source' is what I was described as during this period. I provided others with the energy, confidence and belief they needed to get through. I felt like the lighthouse much of the time; my light was the beacon others needed to get through the storm.

We were all in the same storm, we all had very different vessels.

Mine was very damaged and not many gave us a chance of survival. And the real truth is, no one cares about you and your boat, unless you get it back to shore safely.

This book shares the secrets of some really inspirational people, some of whom are as challenged as you are. Reading this, they are great at giving good advice, they are great at focusing us. Yet, at times, their own lives are equally challenging. I was once told, take people's advice with a grain of salt but be kind with those dispensing it. The advice from the people in here is gold dust, it forms the playbook for anyone running a business or looking to improve the life they have.

The words from Jordan Belfort, the Wolf of Wall Street; Alison Levine, who climbed Everest; Wim Hof, The Iceman; Tim Grover, who coached Michael Jordan; Tim Storey, who was coach and mentor to the Hollywood elite; and Chester Elton, who is the king of gratitude. Adrienne Bankert is the Queen of Kindness; Chris Voss negotiated with terrorists for a living; JJ Virgin and Eric Edmeades were experts in diet and wellness. And so many others offered hope when we were most hopeless.

You will learn brain science, kindness, and appreciation from titans of their industries. It's hard to believe we have captured so many wonderful stories, anecdotes, and tips for success.

Despite everything, I still managed to get the family away for multiple trips. The virus was not going to stop me living my life, and it was the first time many expensive destinations became affordable. It was the tonic I needed to get through, to clear my mind, and find a way to turn our sinking ship around.

In 2020 I spent six amazing weeks in the USA, despite no entry visas from Europe, I found a way, there is always a way, and applied under the hardship visa. This allowed me time with our US business, to help the business stabilize, then recover. I also discovered that many countries (apart from Singapore) allowed waivers for business owners to salvage their business interests. The time in the States gave me moments alone to think, to be creative, and to brainstorm with people who were kind and generous with their time and advice.

Thinking time is so important. Amid any challenging time, find moments to get out of the problem, spend time using a different part of your brain than the one that is 'trying' to solve the problem. I spent much time sitting and thinking about how I could run a better business, what that business was all about, what it would look like, and what we would do differently. And at the end of it, I had a formula for success. I promised myself at the end of this saga/adventure I would behave very differently to the way I went in. No more first in, last out, no more allowing myself to be stressed out by people and situations. I promised myself, I would focus on not wasting a single day.

Some consultants recommended I burn the business to the ground and start again. In some ways, that's sort of what we ended up doing. We changed focus, we performed a transformation, made some great acquisitions and played a long game, while focusing very closely on the scoreboard. Even at the time of publishing (early 2022), I felt like we were only in the third quarter of this pandemic. There are a lot more challenges to come. Also, new problems seem to be daily occurrences. From invasions, chip shortages, logistics issues, and staff who just do not want to come back to work. The cost of living is rising so fast, which is really worrying me. Right now, I am not sure what is going to fix this but know this: things will get better. They always do.

Early in the pandemic, I remember getting an email from a senior investment adviser, telling us that the world could withstand this virus and it would be a short blip, and was nothing much to worry about. How the intelligent, so-called experts got so much wrong is laughable. Our esteemed leaders and scientists messed with our lives and livelihoods. We stayed in, we locked down, and fought over toilet paper and flour. They closed the houses of prayer and education – not even the wars had managed that. The streets were quiet, the roads were empty, the birds sang loudly, and we all wondered what would come next. I cancelled my anniversary trip to Boracay, and the headlines got worse. I was meant to take my top fifteen people to the North Pole: that went the same way. The airlines refused refunds and things started to get worse very quickly.

Nobody believed this would last for more than a few months, the most pessimistic said it would be gone by the end of 2020. And yet two years later, we were all still wearing masks on planes, having to take tests to go anywhere, and America had only just opened again to the world. Two years of hell. It was important not to waste the crisis. With hindsight, I could have taken decisions earlier, and even in 2022 I am fighting battles with people and corporations that think we didn't deliver. People have gone from being experts in covid to experts in war, who knows what they will be experts in next.

For a short period, the world was filled with kindness and care for each other. We walked, talked, and gave back. The high point for me was paying it forward by paying for a nurse's shopping. She burst into tears in the shop which just goes to show that something which doesn't impact you much can make a huge difference to someone else. That was the moment that gives me the fondest memory of 2020 as I look back at the year. We all will have different memories of the pandemic. Some companies were printing money; it was the greatest transfer of wealth in such a short period, especially to the already billionaire digital businesses.

As the months passed, we battled with riots, racism, and rudeness. We all lost hope. We thanked the health workers and front-line staff. We were grateful, gracious, selfless, selfish, and hopeless at the same time.

The governments softened the lockdowns and let us out. We went traveling, had parties, university campuses were war zones and the virus got worse, and so they locked us down again. The scientists ran the countries.

People revolted, people resisted, people moaned and marched. They protested and complained about everything. We went from a period of kindness to hatred and then we had the US election. That opened a whole new can of worms. The people protested a rigged election, did he win, did he cheat. Right wing, left wing – I kept reminding people that planes need both wings to fly. In the end, the craziness came to an end. People ignored much of the good stuff that had been achieved, but let's see what the next couple of years brings. It doesn't matter much who is in government, they make lots of promises and fail to deliver on most. Promises to look after the poor and needy. As any good business operator will tell you, you adjust the sails accordingly.

At the time of publishing, we have had four presidents and six prime ministers since 1994 when we started up our company, Ink. One thing you learn as an entrepreneur, you need to adapt. You look at their policies and how they affect you, then adjust and keep moving forward.

This pandemic has caused more problems than any political party ever will. They will try and fail to break up big tech monopolies, they will have no choice but to raise taxes at some point to pay for all the loans they dished out to keep businesses alive. This was a time when vulnerable and frail people and businesses were lost. Unemployment swelled, despite schemes to keep most people in work. Why would you work when you were getting paid more to stay at home? Nothing made any sense. During most difficult periods weak businesses are destroyed, good companies survive, and great companies come out in a better state than they went in. I feel Ink came through this much better than it found us. In any period of difficulty, opportunity is hiding, and if you look closely enough you will find it.

In my previous book, *There is no F in Sales* I talked about how companies blamed 9/11 and the financial crisis for the failure of their businesses. Yet they were nowhere near New York, or in a market affected by the crisis. My motivation for surviving this period came from the Cantor Fitzgerald story. If you do not know the name Cantor Fitzgerald, they are an Investment Bank, and their HQ was on the 101st floor of the World Trade Center. At 8:46am on September 11, 2001, they lost 66% of their NY staff and by rights should not have been able to survive as a business. Yet, some twenty years later they are still going strong and raise money every year for the relatives of those who perished. If a business that took a direct hit right at the center of that atrocity could survive, then so could we.

The pandemic served us up a direct hit, travel and media were at the center of the storm. We were lucky, none of my team had been lost; we had many youngsters who caught the virus early on who all made a good recovery. As a business, we produced media for airlines, airports and travel companies. The airlines were grounded, the airports shut their doors, and our advertisers were forced to close up.

How do you survive when you cannot sell? In my industry, we sell on the back of people flying, traveling, and corporate travel, this becomes impossible when no one is allowed to fly.

In the past twenty-six years, we had never encountered a time when people were unable to move freely. In every previous crisis, the airlines dropped their prices and people flew. Our story to investors over the years was how this business, despite being dependent on advertising, was immune to recessions and difficult times. Not this time. This time we were in deep shit and reliant on our cash.

I have long understood that cash is king. Forget profit, if you don't collect your cash, you are in trouble.

Having had a really good couple of years, we were very cash-flow positive. We had enough money to ride this out, six months and we would be back in business, that's what the clever sages told us. They were wrong.

When I wrote *There is no F in Sales* in September 2019, I did not realize the impact that title would have on us. Here we were, six months later with no F'in sales. We went from ten million dollars a month to zero. And it wasn't coming back anytime soon. We didn't qualify for loans from the government, so we were very much on our own. We were lucky we had cash, a healthy balance sheet, a supportive investor, and most importantly, a great workforce who in the main supported the business through.

We went from five offices to over 250 very quickly as the world started working from home. Zoom, the FANG stocks, and anyone else who benefited from a work-at-home business model rocketed. Bezos became the wealthiest man in the world. Small and medium-sized businesses went to the wall, others were propped up with furlough monies and bounce-back loans, praying for a miracle to survive. The stock markets collapsed and recovered very quickly and continued to rise, they seemed oblivious to what was really going on. At the time of publishing it's sitting at an all-time high. The TV screens were covered with the number of deaths every day. The narrative was negative, it just got worse and worse. Fear was running through everyone. I was not prepared to participate, same as I had decided in the previous recessions and crises.

Airports closed their doors and we all were unsure what was happening around us. There was no playbook, no manual on how to deal with this type of situation – no formula to follow.

So, in March 2020 I looked in the mirror and said, "What can I do?" What do you do when the rule book doesn't exist? When there is no previous or precedent?

You make up your own rules and create your own playbook.

This is my playbook. You can adapt this to any

difficult situation, it will work. I closed my eyes and went to bed that night. The world was about to change, and no one had any idea of what was about to happen. When I woke up, my head was hurting – how was I going to keep over 170 salespeople engaged and energized, and keep their heads in the game? If I learned anything from the previous catastrophic events we had been through, it was to look after your people, and use this time to recruit from companies who were not doing so. My job was to do just that.

What do you do when all around you are filled with anxiety and worry? How should you think, when the leadership of countries is non-existent? March 2020 was like no other, it became a crisis of communication, a crisis of inconsistency and misdirection at every turn. First, we were going for herd immunity, then we weren't. Sweden went a different way, as governments all had a different message and solution for their people.

All I knew was I had to do something to keep sane, to be able to come out of this with a business.

They, whoever they were, kept saying this would be all over in four to six months. We could not do anything to start the airlines up, the only thing I could control was costs and keeping the team and staff engaged. We managed to keep most of our team whole through to June, we let very few go.

Our goal was to keep everyone together and come out the other end.

I started to ring round, emailing my friends for help. What transpired was a genuine desire to support me and Ink. I didn't have anything to offer other than IOU to be used at some future date, I promised I would support them in any way I could with their missions. Of all the people I reached out to, I had just three people say no. One speaker didn't show, and the odd speaker did a couple of sessions. Everyone who participated gave their time so gracefully and some spent an extra hour chatting with my teams. No one asked for a dime. The format was simple; they talked about the things they knew best, and then answered questions from my global teams. Sometimes, the Singapore teams stayed up to midnight to listen to the speakers. And they were the best bedtime stories.

Over the next fifty-seven chapters, I am going to share the messages from each of the speakers, what advice they gave, what stories they told, and what words of wisdom they have for you in the world today. And also, where you can contact them if a situation arises and you need their help in future. I was told, once upon a time, if you want help, go to a busy or important person. They understand the law of reciprocity, they understand the giving and kindness-first mentality. They understand paying it forward and giving back. I can confirm that is true.

In March 2020 we had thirty-six clients, thirty-three magazines, and a fledgling television network. During the pandemic, we completed a transformation. We added a digital advertising division, and we expanded our television company with the acquisition of the gate network at fifty US airports. A business they only sold due to Covid. With hindsight, I don't think we could have performed this dramatic change without the virus. We went from a low-margin publisher to a high-margin media company. It really was a magical turnaround.

When I tell people this story and that I survived, they go, "That's good," or "Okay," or give some nondescript look of that's not a bad achievement. I explain, we went from a run rate of $150 million to nothing, actually minus nothing, as we had to give lots of money back. I lost 100% of my leadership team, half my workforce, thirty of my airline clients, and thousands of advertisers. This is not a story of a blip, this was a fucking disaster.

In life your identity is who you are, what you stand for, and what values you exude. Each one of us has a fingerprint which is unique and identifies us. Here I was in March 2020 – what identity would I choose? Would I be a victim of this situation or could I be the hero?

This is a choice we all face every day, but this time

the stakes were larger and the downside much scarier than normal.

The words and messages from these powerful speakers, who I will be eternally grateful to, helped me have the courage, the belief, and kindness to stay in the race and start collecting trophies again.

Every one of these talks are available for all our employees to watch back. I am lucky to have built a library of amazing content.

Enjoy the stories and anecdotes from the talks in this book and take copious amounts of notes. Reach out and follow all these brilliant people, most of them share so much great free content on their social channels and remember this: being a leader is a responsibility, it's not a title, the same way if you stand in the middle of a car park and call yourself a car, you don't become a car. It's a badge of honor that you wear with pride. You have other people's lives in your hands and your responsibility is to change their lives and leave them better than you found them.

3

IT STARTED WITH ERIC

MARCH 25, 2020

A conversation with
ERIC EDMEADES

WHEN ERIC CONFIRMED, I had no idea he would be the first of so many great talks. I met him when we climbed Kilimanjaro together in early 2012. He is the founder of *Wildfit*, a wellness company for which he had received the Senate 150 Award from the Canadian government for his work to improve people's lives. He is a worldwide speaker on health, wellbeing, business, and behavioral change.

Eric promised to share core principles of how to keep mentally and physically healthy. This was not just advice for a pandemic, but advice for a long and healthy way of life. It's been Eric's personal mission to get people off medications and using the right foods for wellbeing. This was never more appropriate than during this time. It was still very early in the pandemic and the advice given to us was well ahead of the media.

"Do not look back on this period with any regret, this is a moment in time for you to find you. This is a time for personal growth and development...

People were living in either hysteria or denial. Two dangerous ends of the curve. The virus created unnecessary stress, through lack of movement and lockdown. Stress suppresses the immune system. The press and media were causing fear and this was not helping. Headlines were written that filled us with fear and harmed our immune system.

It was a self-propelling problem. Our bodies were designed and built for a different time. How many times had we received a piece of paper in the mail, be it a writ or bad news, and it activated our fight or flight programs? It's only a bit of paper, yet the effect of it is to make us take action. It's what our minds do, it's what drives our behaviors and thinking.

How many of us have faced actual death? [The answer from our group was about 20%.]

I faced this in a casino in the Bahamas when gunmen burst in and started shooting. Or when I was chased by white rhinos in the bush.

If you go back two generations, everyone faced death, and if you keep going back generations, death was a major issue, with so many facing it in normal life. Today, we do not live in such difficult environments. My experience is that those who have faced a near-death experience are more stoic than most and can handle most experiences better than others.

It is our job to support our bodies physically and psychologically with as much grace as we can. Why? Because we need to, for those around us. We need to be the uplifters of our circle. We need to manage our state of mind and be beacons of positivity. Kids who grew up during the great depression, watching their parents' worried outlook with a scarcity mindset, ended up with a set of beliefs and mindset of being poor or very protective over money. Many didn't buy nice houses or cars and it took decades to change this thinking.

What you do and how you behave during this time will have an effect on you and those close to you for years to come.

Here are the essential needs so you can work towards optimal health and happiness.

- **AIR** – the quality of air, and how you breathe. When you breathe deeply your body knows you are safe.
- **WATER** – drink water.
- **ENERGY** – good quality food – don't buy crap food.
- **SLEEP** – you need more sleep – switch off your devices before you go to bed, nothing is that important. If you need a nap during the day, take it.
- **MOVEMENT** – get out and move – sitting on your arse, your

lymphatic system switches off. Get up every hour. The brain switches off when you don't move.

- **SUNLIGHT** – too much sun is bad for you. But you need - and will benefit from - natural sunlight, even through the clouds.
- **NON-ENERGY NUTRIENTS** – We need amino acids, vitamin C, healthy fats.
- **PHYSICAL TOUCH AND AFFECTION** – we need hugs.
- **SOCIAL CONNECTION** – we need to talk and debate.
- **SOCIAL IMPORTANCE** – we need to feel part of something bigger than us.
- **VARIETY** – we need different things all the time.
- **FAITH** – we need to believe in something.
- **GROWTH** – we need to feel like we are moving forward.
- **CONTRIBUTION** – we need to feel like we are contributing to the greater good."

- ERIC EDMEADES

Remember the workout montage in the Rocky movie where we watch six weeks compounded into two minutes? Eric encouraged us to design our own pandemic montage. What will be the shot list of your movie? Who do you want to be at the end of this event? Human beings are hardwired for a sense of achievement.

As a company we all created our montages, and some of us have these on our desks still. This was the time to learn new things, write that book. Don't do whatever you do every January and break all the promises you make to yourself. Everybody is on pause, you won't fall behind; eat well, get fit, play an instrument and stick to it.

Make sure your kids or family members remember this event as a super fun time, when you got to spend time together and enjoyed that time. We have to bring our super consciousness to the fray. I did this in abundance. I listened and I hope my family and colleagues appreciated this. We did the coolest stuff.

If you have never experienced true hardship, you have no idea what good might look like. It is why at Ink we look for people who have been through stuff and need someone to believe in them. I want you to live a present that the future you will look back on with pride.

Some ideas to help you feel good:
- Order a meal for a first responder, pay it forward.
- A cold bath before you sleep will give you a good night's sleep.
- Thinking about tomorrow positively before you go to sleep will also give you a good night's sleep and you will wake up positively.

Eric left us feeling empowered and energized. We all have a part to play in making sure life is as good as it can be, and I personally picked up many wonderful ideas from this talk that I include in my daily routines. I have been documenting my months ever since this talk, it keeps me accountable every single day of the year, and I find myself wasting very few.

If you want to learn more about Eric, visit *ericedmeades.com*

4

A CONVERSATION OF GRIT

MARCH 26, 2020

A conversation with
SHANNON HUFFMAN POLSON

IT WAS EARLY MORNING in Seattle, as Shannon arrived on screen. She looked like she just stepped off the set of Top Gun. All that was missing were the aviators. If you look up grit in the dictionary, there is a picture of this woman.

Shannon succeeded in what was traditionally a man's world. She was the first woman to fly the Apache attack helicopter, and did many tours with the US army overseas.

This was early in the pandemic, so we didn't really know what was coming. She began by telling us about one of the first conversations she had with her commanding officer.

"Sitting behind a huge desk, we shared pleasantries and before we had finished, he leaned back, looked at me directly in the eye and said, 'You realize that you will never fly an attack aircraft?'...

So I looked back at him and said, 'Yes, Sir'. Because there are times that's the only thing that there is to say.

Does anybody know which way you take off in the Apache helicopter? By the way, it's fifty-eight feet long, twelve feet high, and eighteen feet across. Well, if you are ever in a situation when you have to know this, you turn the nose to face the wind. The resistance will help you to rise. When facing tough times, the only way to come through is to turn to face the wind.

We must own our own stories and control our own narratives.

I did not listen to the CO and took control. I was not about to let that colonel tell me what I could or couldn't do. Because who was I not to fly that thing? After training, I made sure that in the graduation picture I was sitting in the front row – owning my own story.

Yet, there were still obstacles in my way. Newly trained,

I went to Fort Bragg, North Carolina – the tip of the spear as it's the army's base which is ready to deploy anywhere in the world within eighteen hours. I was not assigned to the platoon I wanted, and I'm sure it was because the platoon would have given me a chance to fly and to be an aviation leader. Instead, I was assigned as the assistant to the assistant operations officer and was typing up the annex to operations orders, not even the operations orders themselves. Essentially, doing a lot of typing. One day, a captain looked at me and said, 'Lieutenant, the army doesn't owe you anything'.

One weekend on base, a major I was working for spoke to me and said, 'Don't worry, Lieutenant, you'll be married by the time you're twenty-five'. So I went to see him the next week and said, 'Sir, listen, I'm going to keep doing the best job I can, and I will fly an Apache'. He looked a little surprised. And then he assigned me one additional duty after another.

Why was I typing up the annexes and operations orders? I would ask myself. I'm here to fly the Apache helicopter, to serve my country, and I was there to serve.

Owning your own story doesn't stop at one instance. It's repeated.

It's deciding that you're in control of your own narrative. My personal story illustrates this. My father and stepmother were killed by a grizzly bear on a kayaking trip in Alaska. They had been celebrating their sixteenth anniversary. The bear came into their campsite and they were both killed. Everything that I knew about my life up until that point really shattered in that moment, it seemed like everything stopped.

I hope that will always be the most difficult moment of my life and the most difficult weeks and months and even years that followed it. I captured all these moments in my book North of Hope: A Daughter's Arctic Journey.

It's really about taking that event and working to transform it. I asked myself, from this horrible, terrible and impossible experience, how could I own the narrative and make something beautiful out of this? That's what we have to do with our stories. Aspects of our story we can't control.

Leadership does not have to do with your rank, your position, the number of direct reports you have or don't have; leadership has to do with deciding to be a leader. And that means leading through times of change and challenge. That means leading through resistance. That means we can do anything, it doesn't have to do with what your position is, it has to do with making the decision for excellence, making the decision to be a leader. That's what a leader is. So, this is something to remember if you're in charge of a team, you're in charge of a group in any sense. And you can help your team drill down into their core purposes, each one of them individually. Now, this is before you connect them to the mission of your organization.

> Owning our own stories, deciding to take control of our own narratives is something that we always have the opportunity to do. It's our responsibility to do, to be able to participate in this world, to be able to make this world a better place and to live into the purpose that we really have.
>
> My outcome – I did fly the Apache."
>
> **- SHANNON HUFFMAN POLSON**

All these stories of determination rested in my mind as I faced countless hurdles in the months to come.

To control and own our stories we need to be able to reflect on the things which happen to us and give them meaning. To help do this, follow this exercise. We're going to make a lifeline. Draw a line horizontally on a piece of paper; one end is the start when you were born. Along the line, write out little bullet points for everything that was positive in your life and everything that was challenging. They can be family events; they can be professional events.

Identifying things that had a positive influence on you and things that had maybe a less-than-positive or a negative influence. As you go through this exercise you will see those things which define your life; you have the opportunity to then be able to take those parts of your life and define the narrative you are placing on those moments. Do this today.

When we own our own story, it's not about putting something away and not acknowledging it. It's about the opportunity to take those moments, to transform them into the place that you want to go. Put things together. You have your positives and you have your negative events that go through your life. The next step is to start to see what matters in those events, what values start to come out from them, what starts to be really important, and how experiences that are both positive and negative make you stronger.

How can they teach you to be better? Go back to the things that were the most challenging, that you did get through, and ask yourself how it is that you've handled those, what were the things that you drew on – they might be strengths that you develop later. Identify what those points of strength were, and then apply those to your current situation. There's a parallel between negative and positive events. You decide whether that's something you're going to take forward to get through the hardest times. We take the negative, and we say: what can we take from that? How do I learn from that? How do I take that?

You need purpose and grit. From Shannon's own experience and research, the definition of grit is multifaceted; it's passionate perseverance for the long-term goal, it is dogged determination in the face of difficult circumstances, a refusal to quit in the midst of difficulty, it's that refusal to give in and that refusal to quit. It's at the intersection between your core purpose and your passion.

This is something where you're peeling back the onion, you're really trying to understand what that root cause is. Grit is something you need every single day and when you do the work to drill down to your core purpose, you can find that grit.

You need to be disciplined. Train for grit in the same way as you train for a marathon. You train for one by running. Train for challenges and you train for grit, by doing things that are increasingly difficult, or a little bit more challenging. Then you can pull from those experiences into other challenges to be able to apply that grit. I found myself referring to this talk a lot; I needed grit during this period and there were so many reminders in here.

Drill down into your core purpose and then you can get through anything. For drilling down into understanding your core purpose ask yourself Why? five times. People that are connected to their core purpose are more resilient, produce better results, and have greater longevity. How do you identify your core purpose? Asking why is a great place to start. Why am I here? Why am I here to do this?

You must own your own story. Take control of your own narrative, and you never let that go; you don't give that up to anybody. You need to be realistically optimistic, have a realistic perspective on your circumstance, but always looking towards the future with faith.

We all love a good story and Shannon left us with this thought: we are the authors of our own stories and lives. We are the central characters, we have a beginning, a middle and should always have the ending in mind. When you get to the final chapter, don't let other people write the dialogue for you.

Shannon's talk was a wonderful reminder of that 'never say die' attitude that I have had all my life. I don't care when people say NO to me in business, it just means not now, and that the story I told was not powerful enough to get a yes.

"Remember my story," she told us.

Shannon's book *The Grit Factor* is a wonderful read.

5

THANK YOU FOR YOUR SERVICE

MARCH 31, 2020

A conversation with
SANYIKA 'FIRESTARTER' STREET

IF, THROUGHOUT THIS PANDEMIC, I have bonded with anyone, it has to be Sanyika. At six foot eight, he became my big strong friend through this challenge, and he was delighted to help me rebuild from the start. I have watched him change and grow through the pandemic and I know he helped me, but in return, we have kept each other on point.

He started out single and by the end of 2021, he was a married man with two children. We won an award for the mini movie he produced alongside Ink called A Whole New World, which released in December 2020 and came from one of our many conversations. Today, he and I meet every other Tuesday to inspire each other to be better versions of ourselves.

When Sanyika started the talk in his wonderful storytelling voice, he shared a beautiful poem he had written for the team, setting the standard for these talks. It was called Thank you for your Service.

"When people ask why I get called the 'Firestarter', I explain, one of the first innovations in our time was the discovery of controlled fire. And so, one of the first leaders of our time was literally the person that started the fire. That person was a fire starter...

For thousands of years, we gathered around the fire as a community and shared stories; this ancient tradition of storytelling is my gift to you.

To tell and listen to great stories, we need to be present and grounded and centered. A tactic to do this is to close your eyes, get comfortable, and relax. Then take one deep breath, count to three, hold it, and exhale; one, two, three. Say, 'I am grateful to be here with you'. It's all about being present; that's the most important thing we must give when listening to stories. It's about showing up.

We become greater versions of ourselves when we listen to people, and we are being present for them. Your presence becomes the most powerful gift that you can offer someone in the moment. Don't underestimate the value of simply showing up. It is a valuable gift. You say, 'I'm listening to you'; 'I am present with you'; 'I hear what you have to say'.

I like to ask the question, 'Whose story is the most important to be heard?' and the answer is obvious, other people's. Theirs is what we need to hear. We need to hear what they have to say, what's in their heart, the pain that they're experiencing.

Because then as you transition into your stories. Those stories are going to empower them with the information that's going to help them to see a vision of the future that we are creating and then take them to where it is that we want them to be.

How do we use this in sales? Powerful questions, listening, and speaking to their pain. One of the most important things that you can do is ask powerful questions, and asking powerful questions is at the outset of every great opportunity to tell a story. You need to find out what they're going through, their experiences. We want to reflect on them, what it is that they're experiencing. How they have been addressing that thus far. Then listen, allow for the silence to come, listen to what they are experiencing. The third thing is that you need to speak to their pain.

Speak to what it is that they're currently experiencing, speak to the pain of what they're going through, and let them know that you are equipped to help them navigate through these times. You can help them transition from where they're at to where they want to go. You are there to help them recover. Give them your heart, give them your love. Give them your empathy, be in the present moment with them.

Let me tell you my story. I fell into a depression. I was broke. I was broken financially, broken emotionally. I call it a rock bottom sandwich because I was already at rock bottom, and then rock bottom fell on my rock bottom and then, I was just compressed in between two rock bottoms. I realized that something needed to change.

I got a sales job, working in an industry where we helped people with debt management and their credit. Day one, they wanted one deal a day and to make at least 125 calls; we'd be on the phone for maybe five hours. I started that job with a mindset that I was going to restart my life, this was my chance, and the past was behind me. I thought, I have a real chance to turn my life around. I started off slow. I got three deals in my first two weeks. December was my first full month, and I became the number two salesperson in the entire country.

How? I studied every single night, like my life depended on it. I studied the sales scripts and knew them like the back of my hand. I learned who the client was, what they were experiencing, the pain that they were going through. I knew the objections. I asked everyone for help. I downloaded calls and listened to calls at home. Hearing the way that people transitioned out of objections and how they transitioned using stories.

More importantly, I learned the value of stories. Through listening to their stories, I understood what their vision of the future was and how they wanted me to help with the recovery. We were talking about long-term goals and how they would like to come out the other side.

I found that right after we've listened to them and we have spoken to their pain, we can help them see the future, and the way that we help someone to see the future is by believing that the future is real.

WE MUST BELIEVE IN THE FUTURE.

Do you believe in the future, write your story in one or two sentences of your vision of your future? Where are you going in this moment so you come through this period? How much money are you making? Where are you living? What does your life look like? What are you doing? That future has to vibrate out of you. It doesn't show up in the KPIs, it doesn't show up in the metrics, it doesn't show up in the bottom line. It's an energetic vibration.

Let me tell you, I didn't have a strong relationship with my dad, so I decided to reach out to him. He called me back a week later, and the very first thing that I said to him on the phone was, "Hey, how are you doing, Sir?" He responds, "I'm good." And then he starts talking to me about this new business project that he's working on! We haven't talked in eight years, and the very first thing that he's choosing to have a conversation with me about is a new business venture that he's working on! He didn't listen, he didn't care about my pain. He didn't care about what it was that I was going through. All he cared about was speaking into the space.

He should have acknowledged what I was feeling and been present with me in that moment. The most beautiful thing that he could have done in that moment was to be honest, because as soon as you do that you build trust. My father had in that moment the opportunity to build trust that I could be safe in his space. He didn't.

I started to realize the power of community, the importance of collaboration, and the value of building relationships. It takes a village, and we are a community. We all need to be present, we are an extension of hundreds of other people. And we need to look at how we can collaborate and work together in this moment.

I want to operate from a space of abundance and possibility. When we're going through fear and anxiety, stress shuts us down.

And my final story of opportunity. A janitor shut down his entire business when Covid hit, as a result of the fact that he was in a stressful state and couldn't see the possibility. He didn't see that he had the opportunity to become a hero. He just needed to tell himself a different story. Okay, stores would be closed, and his janitorial service would suffer. He needed to feel that this was an opportunity. He had to change the approach to his story, and that's what he did; then suddenly, his service became the most in-demand service – everyone wanted cleaning. He's no longer living in stress. Suddenly, he has the opportunity to be open and available to what's possible.

So, the reason I'm telling you that story is because stress and anxiety will prevent us from being able to see what is possible. People can feel that it is an opportunity, or that it is a challenge. And both are right. What I feel is that whether it's an opportunity or a challenge, it is your responsibility to move."

- SANYIKA 'FIRESTARTER' STREET

Today, he lights the fire in the bellies of leaders all around the world. You can reach Sanyika at *theallinceo.com*

6

APRIL 2020

A MONTH INTO THE PANDEMIC. Well in the UK and US, longer elsewhere. We are having singsongs every Friday on Zoom, reflecting what we have learned each week from the speakers. The morale seems strong, I am predicting by September we will be back to normal.

My Instagram feed is full of my Starbucks mug collection. If I can't travel, I can dream of places I wanna go visit. It's mad, only six weeks earlier I had teams traveling all over the world, having incredible fun. My Virgin team were in NY, the Miami team were in our studio in LA and learning in Laguna Beach; with hindsight, they all came back a little sick from that trip, maybe they had the virus and didn't even realize it. The German team flew to California and sat on the Friends sofa in LA also. I had just been to the Super Bowl in Miami.

How could the world turn so quickly? This was a time when we all stopped. Our health was now our priority. Our teams' wellbeing was my priority. The mental health situation was bad, people were fed up being at home. The news on TV was full of how many had died today. We had so much time, but most did very little with it. It was still early in the pandemic, and no one had any idea what was ahead of us. The narrative was just so negative and unhelpful. I just kept reaching out to people to help me find more speakers to inspire us and keep us sane.

I started to realize that it wasn't just my teams who were getting inspiration from these talks, but I was really getting lots of ideas on how I could be better, live better and improve aspects of how I ran the business. I needed to ensure I didn't waste this crisis. I needed to look after my wellbeing, and my sleeping and diet needed to improve. I think that's when I started consuming liters of celery juice daily. It was clear that I didn't allow all the negativity to seep in too deeply to my own psyche. I was more aware how powerful 'No' was becoming, and I needed to be able to overcome the negative energy that was everywhere. I needed the grit Shannon had talked about, and also needed to improve my own ability to tell stories, if I was going to get through this.

The lineup for April was so good; my notepad was ready, and I was open and ready to receive the learning.

7

A W1NNING MINDSET

APRIL 2, 2020

A conversation with
TIM GROVER

TIM HAD PREVIOUSLY coached me, and as a favor he offered to help the whole group. He has a unique style, says it how he sees it, and holds nothing back. This event was from the man who made Michael Jordan relentless, and he shared with us how.

The guys were excited for this one. Louie in Singapore had his Jordan t-shirt on and all his books on his table.

Tim told us there were no 'sprinkles' in this talk, "I'm going to tell it as it is!"

"The best of the best don't need motivation, they don't need rah-rah. They don't need 'Let's go'. They need to know where the fuck they're going...

It's not my job to make you feel good. It's not my job to make you happy. You must take ownership; you have to create your own happiness. Because if you can create your own happiness, you can create your own success. You're always looking for the next thing, what to do. It's your responsibility to be able to light that fire inside yourself and keep it lit.

Simon impressed me with his relentless focus to run the Singapore marathon with just five days' training. If I was in Vegas and getting odds for him to finish, boy would I have gambled! Fuck, that guy was in control of his mind and body.

We are all in a race – especially during the pandemic – and in every difficult situation, what we should be asking ourselves is: are we going to finish this race or not? We don't always know where the finish line is, but it's the commitment to completing the race which counts. Give up or partake, finish or don't. Don't just talk about it and what you are going to do – show with the results. Are you willing to do what others won't do and can't do during these times or any time in the future?

We all need to understand that the only real competitor we have is time. The free time that we have can easily distract us. We can wake up in the morning and think the virus is still going on, no one's spending any money. I made all these calls and got nothing, or I didn't make all these calls, damn. How is that thinking going to help you? Is it going to give you a relentless mindset? No, be in control.

There is a lot of chaos in the world, and we are letting the chaos come into our minds. You're letting it come into your day, you're letting it come into your environment. We start to create the chaos. Every time you turn on the news, every time you pick up the phone you have to eliminate the chaos, you must eliminate it from entering in your head. When you don't have idle time, there is less chance of chaos entering.

After all, what you guys do isn't normal. It's not something your parents taught you when you were young, they teach you at school not to talk with strangers and here you are picking up the phone and talking to hundreds of strangers a day. Now, it's about mindset and mastery. Time for you to have mastery of the concept, this is the time to figure out what adjustments you have to make. This is the time to master the application, the execution to adjust and overcome, to achieve the results you want.

You need to work hard. You need to show up early, you need to show up, you need to stay late. Know the harder you practice, the easier the game will be. Hold yourself accountable. Control the situation. As an example, if you see somebody who is not making their calls and not selling but they have a list, say, 'Hey man, give me that list. I'll make the calls'.

On a call, when a person says 'no,' or 'this is not the right time,' before you go on to the next number, review the call, jot down a little note next to that number about why you didn't close that deal. In basketball, 'I know why my guys made the shot' – the skill is in knowing why they didn't make the shot.

It wasn't about blaming; don't put the blame on the other person because that's the easiest way to do it. You can't blame it on the rim. You can't blame it on the basketball, you can't blame it on the environment. The rim is ten feet tall; the basketball is the same size and there is the same amount of air in the air conditioning or the heat inside of an arena. So, you need to eliminate the excuses.

Drills and practice are the key. Not only did my athletes have to make the basket, but they also had to make the basket in a certain way. Like you had to make one hundred shots that didn't touch anything. Let me explain how I think 'making baskets' is like making telephone calls. It's all about drills. For every missed basket, there's a reason behind it.

Change your focus from, 'I have to make five hundred calls,' and rather, focus on making two hundred calls the right way. Remember the burpees challenge that went around? You had to do one hundred burpees, but people that were doing those burpees had absolutely terrible form, they were so worried about doing them in the time that they did them badly. It's the same for you; you make five hundred calls in a certain time, yet you are doing them with terrible form. Do it in the right way, move from managing time, to embracing and managing focus.

When you control the situation, there's actually more pressure. When you get into an argument with somebody, somebody is screaming at you, it takes more control, takes more stress or pressure not to snap back at that person. It is more pressure on you, because you have to control certain situations that you didn't have to control before, especially during the pandemic – having to work home, around your kids, and the forced challenges of business.

This is not a time to be overly emotional. This is a time to know exactly what your self-worth is. This is your 'watch me' moment. People want to be watched when things are going well. When things are going bad, they don't want to be watched, because that's when you get exposed."

- TIM GROVER

I loved this, and every time I was having a bad moment, I would think, who is watching me, got to get out of this. It was hugely motivational.

Sadly, the talk was coming to an end. Tim left us

with this thought. Think about it, when this is over, there's something else coming. Be ready and prepared. And he was spot on. Ukraine, Yemen, it's never ending.

On my phone, I have a video of Tim telling a group the story about my marathon exploits. Any time I feel a little down, I watch that back as a reminder of how powerful I am and continue to be.

From now on, put expectations on yourself, and they should be way greater than what anyone else can put on you. In fact, they need to be of a higher standard than anybody else.

Tim's book, *W1nning* was so powerful and launched at just the right time for me and my senior team to get that winning mindset back. If you love winning, it's a must-read.

8

LET'S CREATE A FUTURE WE LIKE

APRIL 8, 2020

A conversation with
JB THE WIZARD

IN EARLY 2020, I came across JB. I begged him to work with me. He is one of the most expensive coaches I have ever worked with, but also one of the most incredible and impactful.

I wanted my team to enter the 'world of the wizard'. JB is an award-winning filmmaker and producer, lives in the US, and sounds a bit like Harry Potter. His skill in business is unlocking and getting people's heads out of their bums. It's about being present, authentic, and believable. He's known as the 'chiropractor of the soul' because, in his words, "I am identifying those tiny areas that are holding people back from fulfillment, answers, and mastery in life so that they can all have complete freedom." It's all about futuring - providing value to others through your ability, and to help enough people and know you will be looked after.

As the meeting started, JB, a bearded man, came close to the screen and recited the most beautiful poem. What a way to create engagement.

> ## "I've been an entrepreneur all my life, and never had a salary. And I remember as an aspiring actor not having enough money to pay for gas/ petrol to get to acting classes and auditions. I remember looking for quarters down the back of the sofa...
>
> It was a difficult and challenging time, but I said, "I've got to stand up and make things happen." I had to build my bravery muscle.
>
> He tells us of one audition he went to with a sprained ankle: I couldn't walk and was on medication. Throughout the entire audition, I didn't know what was going on, I was out of it. I could have not shown up for the audition, yet I did. And guess what, surprisingly I got the part.
>
> Your goals and your dreams in everything that you want

are on the other side of safety. Dreams only fade when you stay in the comfort zone and listen to your limiting beliefs. I could have let my sprained ankle get the better of me, I could have had a 'limiting belief'. That limiting belief would have stopped me getting the role and kept me from doing something. And that can happen to us all. We need to understand that a limiting belief has a purpose. It is there to protect us. Think of it like this, a baby beginning to walk; the hands go out to protect them from falling and hurting themselves – imagine the hands are limiting beliefs. Babies don't crawl forever, so there comes a stage when that limiting belief needs to go.

How do we deal with our limiting beliefs?

The first thing we need to do when the belief appears is thank it and appreciate it as it wants to protect us. The next step is to think, do I still need that protection, is it still applicable? And then finally, and most importantly, ask yourself do I still want to have that limiting belief? You then have to take actions to solidify and to prove to yourself that you don't need it anymore.

A limiting belief is most likely keeping you from reaching, accessing, and activating your atomic core. What is an 'atomic core'? This is the reason you're on this planet, it's an alignment of your reasons and your values. There's a reason that you are exactly where you are right now. We all have done many things, and within those many things there's usually a common theme, running through all those things that appear different on the outside. This is part of discovering your atomic core. When you remove everything, what's left? It's just this core thing that you believe in. And what we want to do is activate that reason, we want to discover what that reason is, and then take action as you can ask yourself, what is it that you like? What is it that you're good at? Your atomic core is burning alive, it always has been burning, it always will. It's inside of you. It will never go out until you're finished in this world.

Double down on your strengths and take action. When you do take action, you should always ask yourself, is this action a part of your atomic core? Do you feel that this is going to help you with your reason for being on this planet? If you answer yes, then, you're basically invincible. Because you're being true to yourself. And when it comes to getting things done, something to do that's a bit uncomfortable, or something that you don't like, if you are aligned with your atomic core then you can get through it. Discipline is going to make certain that you're in alignment. Discipline is not forcing yourself to do something that you hate. That's not discipline, that's stupidity.

We do at times have a challenge getting alignment with our atomic core and one reason is self and social pressure. Concerns with how we're going to look if we fail. What if it doesn't work? We want to feel safe; sometimes we've not seen it done before and we think it's not possible. We need to feel like it certainly is and that we're great enough. Say 'I'm good enough'. Think of this, what happens as you walk? It's the mind telling the body to shift itself slightly off balance. And then what happens is one of the feet moves forwards to stop the fall. So really, walking is a constant state of avoidance of a fall – and you mastered that, okay?

This is the most remarkable time for each of you. This is the time when you're able to stop, think, and consider your alignment. This is the time where you're able to take a look at your life, take a look at how it's going. How you're operating it. Do you like it? Is it working for you?

In order to take action, you want to know how and where you should take action. That's where alignment comes in, wanting to act towards things that are in alignment with who you are and what your core is really all about.

Here is a sporting example of alignment. When you play tennis your bones, your muscles, and your tendons have to be aligned. Once they're all in alignment and you hit that ball, it feels like a lot less effort, the ball is going faster, you're feeling good. If you turn your wrist just slightly, or lightly, as you strike the ball, it could put a spin on the ball, and change the outcome of playing. I call them two-millimeter shifts. And those can be the difference between a win or a loss, between winning the trophy and not. This can affect your entire life trajectory, everything can be shifted, it's all about marginal gains. There's a word in the Wizard dictionary, called 'reverse panic'. This happens when many choices were in alignment, and you think back and ask – if I were just slightly out of alignment in that moment, how many things would never have come to be? You are on the cliff face and you almost fall, but you don't. But you still got the adrenaline rush because you almost fell. That's what happens.

You might want to think about 'cloning'; what I mean here is think about the task and activity that needs to get done. Focus on what you're good at and you will notice areas you're not. Here's a personal example: I don't like email, so I don't email, I don't use email, I don't check email. What if using email is essential to my business? What then? So, I paid attention to what I didn't like about it. What am I good at with it? And realized that I needed to train somebody that could do those tasks. This is different to delegating. We delegate too soon, before we are aware of the problems and snags with the task. If we delegate too soon, we might miss a poor job, but we would notice it too late. Time is very expensive, money is very cheap. If the task doesn't energize you then don't do it, and those tasks could be done more efficiently with somebody else investing time in them.

You must play to your strengths and what you are good at to get marginal gains and those two-millimeter shifts. What we want to do is double down on strength, as opposed to simply getting good at the weaknesses. For example, an Olympic speed skater who was very good at the corners, but he wasn't at the straightaways. So, he just focused on getting better at what he was great at - the corners - and guess what happened, he performed so much quicker.

You need a mirror to see the back of your head – obvious, right? I just serve as a mirror to help you to see what you already know.

The goal = learn how to avoid limiting yourself.

We need to wipe away everything that distracts us and get to the core of what it is and be authentic. When I coached public speaking, the biggest problem that I helped people work through was figuring out what they are saying, what they want to say, how they want to communicate, how they can be authentic and how they can be present. I ask them, are you comfortable with what you want to be called? Do you feel comfortable with that title? Do you like how you are being referred to? What do you like being called when you're working? This will begin to identify things in our lives, or our past experiences that were blocking us from moving forward."

- JB THE WIZARD

One-way JB gets two-millimeter shifts is by being aware of his Circadian schedule. Circadian rhythms are twenty-four-hour cycles that are part of the body's internal clock, running in the background to carry out essential functions and processes. As humans, we get into rhythms. These are unique to everyone.

Be aware of yours over the next couple of days; how you feel and what you're thinking about at certain times of the day. If there's an activity that you dread, is there another time of the day that you can do that activity, and either dread it less or even enjoy it? Can you switch it to that time? Your productivity will increase, efficiency increases, the lag on your brain decreases, and it will open you up to seeing things that you were not previously able to see. If you're only doing it because it needs to get done, what's going to happen is you are not going to do it well, and that is going to be very expensive.

Waiting is a victim state.

It's when we don't feel like we have control, don't know what's going to happen next, that's when anxiety creeps in. To move from that state, you need to act towards what you want to be. Any kind of action is better than no action. Walking is better than sitting, running might be better than walking. Adaptation is so important at any time because it's always an opportunity. By the time everything passes it may be too late.

You cannot touch your thoughts; you must translate and transfer them into writing and then they will exist in your reality. When they exist, you need to align them. Release thoughts. Write them down on a piece of paper, that is one of the first moments of you setting out on your new journey. This is such a powerful exercise. The team were blown away by this talk, there were so many powerful nuggets, it was hard to take it all in. I had to watch the talk back a few times.

I adopted the bravery muscle after this talk, it was a real help during the pandemic, find yours and see where it takes you.

JB is on Clubhouse and social media daily, follow him and connect, the man is a genius and a wizard.

9

TIME FOR FAITH, NOT FEAR

APRIL 8, 2020

A conversation with
TIM STOREY

TIM HAS BECOME a good friend; we met a few years ago and instantly hit it off. We sat on the beach in Marbella and waxed lyrically for hours. I knew Tim's session would be good, but it turned out to be weirdly magical. He has coached some of the greatest minds in Hollywood, his stage presence is phenomenal, so I knew this would be a superb performance. It went way beyond what I expected.

Some of the lines from this talk inspire many of the poems I have written, you can check these out *@TheMotivationalPoet* on Instagram.

"I'm not a motivational speaker. I'm an educator. I will push your buttons, and I will shake you up...

I started off with a big dream. We had seven people in our family and a two-bedroom apartment – that's very cramped. I knew that someday my life was going to shine in a crazy, crazy way. But I knew I was going to do more than what I saw.

There are three ways to live:
1. **ALMOST** – close but no cigar
2. **MOST** – a ceiling is set
3. **UTMOST** – the max life

Where do you want to live at? I worked with Robert Downey Jr; Robert said to me, 'Tim, do me a favor. Don't try to make my life great. Just make me okay'. And I remember saying to him, 'I can't do that. I don't do okay, I do utmost'. And Robert got emotional as I would not let him live in the land of okay. He went from being where he was to being Iron Man. Don't get stuck in an almost or most life, because - let me just tell you something - once you touch the fire, you can't live in smoke. Tim then gave us tips for leading an utmost life.

REMEMBER, WE ARE ALL BORN AN ORIGINAL – DON'T DIE A COPY.

There are three ways to enhance learning and education: read books, find amazing people and have conversations, and make observations – see everything around you and live-in awareness.

We all start with momentum. Momentum is an energy or force in your soul.

Start with momentum. When we have life interruptions, setbacks settle and we tend to 'sit in the setback', and some literally cement themselves in the setback and become a discount version of themselves.

You got a calling, you got to rise to the call. Then develop the character for the call. My character started getting built with being raised in a lower-income family. My father died when I was ten in a car accident, then my sister died when I was twelve in another car accident. I had racism against me since I was a kid – all this was character building.

I believe that the struggle I went through and struggles you go through are character building. You got to have courage. I'm not good at quitting, I'm not good at giving up. I told my mother when I was twelve years of age. I said, 'Mom, when I'm in my twenties you will never worry about money again'. Guess what happened? By my mid-twenties! My mother never worried about money again. When I had to answer the call, I had to develop character. Then I had to develop courage.

When adversity comes, some people get disheartened, people get dispirited. A second thing that happens with adversity is fear. Fear, panic, dread, worry, unrest, doubt, disbelief. It's not how we live in an utmost life. I remember one conversation with Magic Johnson, and we were talking about crisis. He's like, 'Come on, Tim. Crap, we've been through loads, that is what we have to do, and know we can get through this and get through this game.' Remember, he was named as one of the fifty greatest NBA players in history.

What tips do you have on dealing with adversity?

There are different levels of adversity. I got this Mini Cooper, and in the first week of driving it I was down the freeway and all of a sudden, a truck with dirt in the back. And I see this boulder just start pounding on the freeway. It comes right at my windshield. Oh, it hits my windshield and creates a crack. Three weeks later, I'm on another freeway, and a guy is driving with a mattress which came off the back of his truck and hit the car.

In life, sometimes a boulder comes at you, or a mattress comes towards your car. Don't get dramatic in the midst of the drama; in adversity you must become aware you have a crisis, you got to take inventory to identify the size of adversity, plan a strategy accordingly and act on it. Then reach for people who are stronger than you. While managing your own expectations and not getting frustrated, focus on the fact that you are moving forward – getting to the other side of the mountain is a process with a clear outcome.

These situations are real, it's a fact. Mindset finds answers. We all have mountains to climb in our lives, they may be physical, mental, a job or finances. There are different ways to get on the other side of the mountain. Sometimes you just drive through the mountain, and sometimes we must scale them. It's important to feed our faith and starve our doubts. Whether it's meditation, prayer, walks, conversations, exercise, being with positive great people, we begin to build our faith, which changes our mindset. It's not just about optimism, those doubts feel real. It's proven that faith and mindset will help us not just to get through adversity, but to find answers. We're looking at, how do I get to the other side if the drama hits? Build faith to a level that you know that you can go through it.

In situations you go through two things at once: recovery and discovery. Don't get caught up in the recovery zone so you miss your discoveries. That's the beauty of life. The beauty of my life has not been in all my decisions. It's in my discoveries. Focus on: 'Feeding your faith and starving your doubts, Mindset will change your mood state'. We need to understand that what we feed our minds with changes our perception of reality, and that is what we need to adjust, the importance of our mindset, to change our mood state. You all will get through this crisis, and whatever is next."

- TIM STOREY

In the questions after Tim's talk, someone asked, "What qualities do celebrities share?" His answer surprised me. "Disappointment," he said. "Everyone goes through disappointment; for every project that succeeds, many fail by the wayside. They get disappointed by people, family, and colleagues just like anyone." He didn't know at an early age that one day he would be hanging out with superstars and helping them with projects.

Tim had a weird knack of looking at people in the Zoom call, and literally in a fortune teller sort of way, telling them what their issues were. I knew all these people and it was spookily accurate. He looked at Gerry and said, "You got a second chance, my friend, don't waste it." Gerry had died briefly in 2015. Tim had no idea about this. He went on to read four or five of my team so accurately. This was a life lesson for many.

Tim's book The Miracle Mentality helped me enormously through the pandemic, he sent me a copy with the most wonderful message. Tim and I are working on a show for our ReachTV network and we meet regularly wherever our paths cross. I am very fond of his teachings, and he is a wise sage, when I need one.

You can follow Tim at *timstorey.com*

10

LIVING IN A STATE OF PERFORMANCE

APRIL 15, 2020

A conversation with
BRAD LEA

I HAD APPEARED on Brad's podcast Dropping Bombs in January 2020. Who knew this pandemic was ahead of us! Brad was a chest-beating, alpha male - or that's how he was perceived by the outside world. The man is as genuine as the day. Who was the first person to call me to see if I was okay when all this kicked off? Brad Lea. "How can I help you?" he asked. Will you come and inspire my team, Brad? "Of course, I will," he replied.

Sat by his pool in the Vegas sunshine, in his true authentic style, Brad tells us his name is Lea, as in tea and not lea-ah. The reality he told us was that you have to have L-E-A or you cannot spell sales – still makes me chuckle typing that.

"The best time to live is right now. When you look in the past, you know you get depressed, and when you look to the future, you get anxious, you have anxiety. In most cases, what you fear doesn't come true...

I believe that all failure comes from the lack of knowledge, and that there are four ingredients necessary if you want to train yourself effectively – good content, repetition, practice, and accountability.

I became a leader in the sector by collaborating. When you collaborate, you get a lot more, and the reason why I believe that is I think the universe has its own little laws and when you contribute to the universe you add more to the universe. People are always asking me if you need a degree to be successful - no, you don't. I don't think there's a secret there. I now have four MBAs, two PhDs, and three master's degrees. They all work for me.

Let me tell you about the million-dollar morning. The reason I call it that is because everyone on this call knows for a fact that if I gave you guys all a million dollars or two million, or even three million cash, no strings attached, you'd be in a pretty decent mood. This helps me wake up every day and it's absolutely the best possible gift. Now, it sounds fluffy and cheesy but think about it. If I give you a million dollars, but said you cannot wake up tomorrow, obviously you wouldn't take it.

If you think logically and you use common sense, opening your eyes in the morning is the equivalent, or better than getting a million dollars every single morning. The first thought in your head every single morning should be, very simply: I just got something worth more than a million dollars. I get it and I wake up grateful.

The million-dollar morning consists of these practices:

1. **FOCUS FIFTEEN MINUTES ON YOUR HEALTH.** Get your blood pumping, move around no matter what and eat something nutritious. Who wants a bunch of money if you can't enjoy it!

2. **READ FIFTEEN MINUTES OF A BOOK,** jump into a course, or learn something new every day if you want to change your behavior.

3. **SPEND FIFTEEN MINUTES MANAGING RELATIONSHIPS.** I'm telling you right now, relationships are everything. If you don't understand how or why, or you think it's using people, or you're too nervous to introduce yourself, well then, folks, you have a problem with yourself. Call five people every single day that you want to build a relationship with, and you want to improve your relationship with. It could just

be acknowledgement. It could just be gratitude, it could just be a message of kindness, it could be anything you want, but do it every day. If you pissed off anybody or you wanted to repair any relationship with anybody, then you know you first should apologize and ask for forgiveness. I've told my wife sorry when I didn't even do anything.

4. **SET TEN SMALL GOALS A DAY AND DO THEM.** Huge goals are half the reason you don't like yourself. Think of it this way; you wanted to make a million dollars and you made six hundred thousand – you are a loser. You can tell yourself whatever you think, like hey, at least I came close, no that's called rationalizing. You fucking lost, people. Achieving ten small goals every day means you are a winner every day, you're winning ten times a day and you may not realize it, but eventually you're going to sit up a little taller. You're going to walk a little more proudly and you're going to think you deserve a little bit more. Intentionally and consciously, experience wins, it's repetition and memory. Everything's experience, so experience winning.

5. **DO FIVE THINGS YOU CAN DO TO DRIVE REVENUE TODAY.** Not this week, today. How do I drive revenue today? Make a call, make a sale, make a close, make a connection, prospect to lead, qualify a lead, do something that drives revenue.

6. **FOCUS ON YOUR MONEY.** Folks, people say that money doesn't buy happiness; they just don't know where to shop.

Believe it or not, we have what's called the subconscious, which means under-awareness, you're not aware of it, but it's there. You've been recording every word, every sound, everything your whole entire life. And after a while, that subconscious mind starts to dictate who you are and what you say and what you think and how you choose the choices you make. The choices you make determine the road you'll take. You can sit there in your home or your flat, depending on where you are, and you can sit there and whine and cry and bitch and moan and complain. Or you can freakin' have a different perspective, be thankful you're alive, get on the phone and meet people. If you cannot do that right now, you can do something. Isn't that awesome, that you have the ability to do something?

I strongly recommend that you go to sleep, wake up early and work your ass off, and make sure that you exhaust yourself throughout the day. Every time I don't work out and I don't work that hard and I'm kind of lounging around, you know, I find myself watching TV till early in the morning, then I can't go to sleep.

What does success look like? If you have to think and you don't know what it looks like, that's a problem. Let me give you an example. You guys know what I look like and sound like, okay, and you walked into a room with only five people in it, and your job was to find me – it would be easy. But how hard would it be to find me in a room full of fifty people? It just takes a little more time, that's all.

You got to figure out what success looks like. The challenge is now about how do we get successful? Let me tell you, there is no key to success. It's a combination of things. If you want to get successful, or you want to change what you're getting, you have to change what you're doing. You have to change your behavior. And if you want to change your behavior, you have to change your beliefs; your beliefs are what drive your behavior.

How do you reprogram your beliefs? You don't. You change your beliefs by adding new information, you must put into it what you want it to learn. It's like a computer, you put into the computer the information you want it to have.

People trade time for money. And then people trade money for time. You know I always got told when I was growing up, 'You better save for a rainy day.' I'm like, 'What's wrong with a sunny day?' Why not just follow the sun so it never rains. However, if you don't understand that money is a tool, and you never use it, well then, guess what? You're going to have less of it. If you're a piece of shit because of money, well then you are a piece of shit without money. Money is not the problem. You don't have to agree that money is important for you, you just have to let go of the fact that money is not important. Yes, it is. It makes a massive difference.

Alcohol is poison, we all know that's correct. Alcohol is poisonous to our body, it is not good for our body, it is not good for anything, it is poison; but yet when we win. What's put in our head by alcohol companies and society? Let's celebrate. Whoo. Let's hurt ourselves for winning. Okay, guys, listen, there's nothing wrong with a celebratory drink, just avoid a celebratory blackout.

The reason I say what I say is because I believe it, and I think it's going to help people, and I'm doing it for the right reasons. I don't need your approval. I don't need people's approval. Too many people fear the judgment of others. And when you fear the judgment of others, you're limiting what you say, what you do, what you think, and what you want. How many people have not done something in fear of what other people might think? That's limiting yourself, why would you limit yourself?

As an example of control, about the pandemic, I don't know what the conspiracies are, but I don't care, I control what I believe. I'm not going to believe all this conspiracy bullshit. I'm going to live in the now and I'm going to decide what's happening with me that I can control right now, because I can control that. I can't control everything and if I control how I react, then I technically have the control, don't I? You get what you tolerate. Write down everything that you don't like in your life and realize that you are tolerating it. You're the one that's choosing it. It all boils down to choices, you're choosing to tolerate what it is you don't like.

So, if you don't want something, just stop tolerating it. I get to decide whether I'm happy or whether I'm pissed, you don't get to decide. If you come up and you say, 'Hey Brad, you're a frickin' dick'. I get to decide whether that bothers me or not. I get to decide whether I have a good day or a bad day. So literally the next time you're having a bad day, remember, you're choosing to have a bad day – stupid. This is so powerful and so many people live with caring too much about what people say and think of them, it doesn't matter.

Be authentic, be yourself and say it the way you see it. Because I've said 'bro', this authenticity has made more deals than it has cost me. One great example, I had business with a church group. Before the meeting, I told my colleague I had to leave the presentation early to go and see the Scorpions, a German heavy metal band, and I was going to mention it to them. He said, 'Oh my god you're kidding me, you can't say that, this guy is a pastor, this guy's a preacher, this guy's, you know, religious! Dude, you're gonna ruin the deal, you're gonna blow the deal'. The first thing I said at the meeting was, 'I'd love to sit here and chit-chat but, man, I've got tickets to the Scorpions'. The pastor said, 'You're going to the Scorpions, I love the Scorpions.' And guess what? We ended up taking them to the Scorpions and we closed a big deal. The moral is: be honest.

And don't worry about what people may or may not be thinking.

Confused minds don't make decisions. Anytime you're confused or anytime you are uncertain, you will hesitate, you will pause, you will procrastinate, you will question, and ultimately, you're second-guessing yourself. And then you start to falter. That's because we have an inherent need to survive. And sometimes second-guessing yourself, it's just being cautious, keeping you safe.

If you want to be more confident, remember confidence is just the memory of winning. Imagine a fighter going into the ring, and every time he kicks everyone's ass. He gets so confident at fighting anyone that wants to fight, he is totally confident to win, it's just the memory of winning. Confidence is the memory of winning. Your subconscious mind doesn't know the difference between a big win and a small win. That is why you need to go get your small wins every day."

- BRAD LEA

And here are some final words of advice from Brad; he shared a lot of good stuff but, "It's up to if you want to listen." As a leading expert in online training, he told us his mission in life is to get the knowledge from the people who have it to the people who need it.

Brad lives up to his mission of sharing information, and his nonchalant approach is a lesson to us all in being authentic and honest, and he has shown us that we don't need to sugar coat things. Tell it as it is. If people don't want to listen, then find people who do. Having a million-dollar ritual and waking up is the greatest value of all.

Throughout lockdown, Brad would check in to see how I was doing. He is straight-talking with a heart of gold.

Brad Lea's podcast, *Dropping Bombs* is a must-listen, his new book *The Hard Way* is great read. *bradlea.com*

11

LEARNING IN THREES

APRIL 16, 2020

A conversation with
DAVID MELTZER

ON MY BOOK TOUR, I met David; he was one of life's good people. He was genuinely interested in helping in any way he could. When I asked him to help, I hadn't even finished the sentence and he said yes.

David, the man behind the motivation for the movie Jerry Maguire, joined us full of beans. He didn't once shout "show me the money." He just gave us sound advice for making the most of our time and changing the world for the better. I decided to bring in my friend, a quick drawing expert, to draw his talk and this appeared all over social media.

His opening story was 'life is a lesson'. He told us of growing up with a single mum, with a black belt in Jewish guilt. He and his five siblings listened to her always, and she invested all her time and energy in her work so they could be educated.

"If I ever came down the stairs without a mindset of gratitude, then I would be sharply encouraged to go back upstairs and adjust my mindset...

We need to be authentic. Despite my mother's good advice, I have seen the danger in trying to please other people because they were friends, family, and associates. Don't make decisions based on family, unless the family member has the experience. Mums will always be great mums, but not always great business decision makers. Always listen, yet be authentic to yourself and in your life. My mum's advice cost me millions. Be careful who you take your advice from.

My mission in life is to spread happiness, it's the most incredible virus ever created! It's the most viral of all viruses, it can be spread simply by witnessing it. My mission in life is to empower over a billion people to be happy. I'll share the math with you: empower a thousand people a thousand times to each empower a thousand people and then we get over a billion. What is happiness? It's the consistent, persistent pursuit of your potential. In other words, happiness is derived by making a lot of money, helping a lot of people, and having a lot of fun.

My drive was that I wanted to be rich enough to make other people rich. It's all about creating options for ourselves, and that's what creates success, and those options are created by enjoying every day without quitting in the pursuit of our potential. I may never see the billion people I have empowered with happiness; the results are exponential and will take time, yet it doesn't stop me. You have to shift from attaching emotions to an outcome – 'I will be happy when...' – to attaching them to the enjoyment of consistency, the persistency and the pursuit of your potential. In other words, learn to love what you do, look for the light, the love, and the lessons. Everything has value, everything can be enjoyable.

I decided that I was going to beat people with math and time, not with talent. If I could speed up brushing my teeth every day, I could save four minutes per day; that was twenty-four hours of productivity a year that I would save. Make a decision; instead of working eight hours being productive today, stay focused and make sixteen hours of productivity a day. You will be twice as efficient. Did you know people waste eighty hours a year looking for things; your wallet, your keys, your cell phone. So, find a place to put your phone, find a place to put your keys, and find a place to put your wallet.

Just make sure that you have an activity that you are being paid for. And avoid being too rigid, stay open to change, and adapt action while you still implement strict scheduling and productivity.

The old view of money that money buys love and money

buys happiness was wrong, because it doesn't. All it does is allow you to shop, and if I shop for the right things like community centers in Africa, Junior Achievement empowering kids with scholarships, then I will be happy. But I can't do it without money, and the best way and the easiest way to make money is sales.

So here are a few things I have learned on my journey about sales:

1. Be more interested than interesting.
2. Always be credible. If you're 100% credible, you don't have to say much more than 'send me your money'.
3. People buy on emotion for logical reasons. Your initial call is to stimulate interest, then transition interest, and finally share a vision. You need emotional attachment to do that.
4. Be confident. If you can't articulate effectively, 'Can you see any reason why you won't want to move forward?' then you're not ready to sell. It's like walking, you can only walk when you know what you are doing.
5. Do you provide more value than you are asking for?
6. In any sale the last thing that is important is the features and benefits of what you're selling.
7. Make sure you are asking a series of open-ended questions: How can I provide value or service? What are you doing today? What do you like about it? What don't you like about it? Would it help you if...?

Some advice to help with performance:

- Take inventory of your values. Don't worry about changing your values either. That just means you're growing and learning. Changing values according to the skills that you've developed and knowledge that you've acquired, maintaining or growing the desire to be what you can be.

- Be a student of your calendar. Pay attention to your calendar, put intention into your calendar. Every day in the morning, at night, study what you have planned. Pay attention and intention to the coincidences you want, what you have planned in your calendar. Study what you don't have planned, study the blank space in your calendar, the white space in your calendar, the empty space in your calendar. When you study with the lens of productivity, accessibility and gratitude, you will become more productive, you'll be more statistically successful, you'll be more effective and efficient with your time.

- Study your sleep. When you get the right amount of sleep and create an adaptable routine, one in which you wake up and utilize your time for maximum productivity, accessibility and gratitude.

- Everything that happens in my life I ask myself – can I do it now? And if I can do it now, I will do it! Why, because 100% of the things you do now get done.

- Understand that fear motivates us, but it doesn't inspire

> us. Fear will get you focused, but it won't last. It only lasts a short time.
> - The greatest athletes, celebrities, and entertainers, they only love a percentage of what they do. The majority of what they do, they have had to learn to love. That's the truth in all of us. Most of us don't learn to love enough of what we do. We change jobs, careers, way too easily."
>
> **— DAVID MELTZER**

And for a bit of fun David shared 'the jerky boys' strategy. The jerky boys would cold call, and they made fun of people, harass and be rude to them, but people wouldn't hang up. So, I would do a training session where I would time people and give a bonus to see who could get someone off the phone the fastest. Now, here's what's interesting. The average time of people getting off the phone was slower than when they were trying to sell to them. Now what does that tell us?

I love the way David uses three words in everything he discusses. Three is important. He uses math to drive systems and processes to deliver better performance and productivity. This helped him make a million dollars in nine months.

If you want to be accountable, simply ask yourself two questions.

What can I do to attract this into my life?
And what am I supposed to learn from it?

Make sure you understand the difference between liability and accountability. If you're hit from behind because someone's texting, don't say to yourself that they're not liable. A blame type of thing, that's man-made, but accountability is much bigger. You still need to ask yourself, what did I do to attract someone hitting me from behind? And what am I supposed to learn from it? If you're looking for the lessons, the love and the light and everything, even from getting hit from behind, it will be an expansive positive in your life.

You can join David for free Friday Training sessions by registering at: *dmeltzer.com/training/*

12

THOUGHTS BECOME THINGS

APRIL 19, 2020

A conversation with
DR. MARK GOULSTON

ONE OF THE PEOPLE who kept me sane during this whole period was my friend, Dr. Mark Goulston. Every Thursday we would have a check-in, and he would challenge and inspire me to keep on going; his advice and listening was invaluable. If you ever read the book Tuesdays with Morrie, mine was Thursdays with Marky!

Mark said often people work with him because they think of him as the big brother they never had. They say, 'You know, you're kind of irreverent. You're funny. You seem smart. And you can hit me right between the eyes with something I don't want to hear, but I need to hear, but it is laced with love'. What an amazing introduction to the man who is Dr. Mark Goulston.

"I live to serve other people, I'm much more famous than I am rich. I never take advantage of people. I never hurt people. It's all about alignment, we are told. Wealth is what you take from the world, worth is what you give back – and if these are your values then consistently live by them.

Sometimes when I visit a company, I will say to the CEO, 'You know, I don't think I want to work with you. I could probably help you, but I don't want to work with you. Because I don't work with a company where anybody is afraid to come to work because of someone else's personality, and you are turning your back on that because you just want to make money. If they're afraid to come to work because you know they're not doing their job, okay, we'll fix that.'

It's about listening. Not just focusing on what people are listening to, but focusing on what they are listening for. The first is just a transactional conversation. The latter is about you delivering on what they are not telling you, getting them to consider what you're saying. [As Mark describes it, 'they lean in' and unfold their arms.] So how do you do that, I hear you all ask?

You create what a 'Whoa, Wow, Hmmm, and Yes' formula. Unfortunately, people are communicating from fear, people are just afraid. So, one of the ways to move them from fear to excitement is to create a 'Whoa, Wow, Hmmm, and Yes' situation. You bring up something that's familiar - that gets you into their mind - and then you give it a twist.

HERE IS AN EXAMPLE:

How many of you have ever seen the FedEx logo on a truck?

Now how many of you know the secret of the FedEx logo?

It's the arrow between the E and the X. And now, once you see it you will not miss it. You will open people's minds, you create a "Whoa, I can't believe what you just told me. I can't believe what I'm hearing. I can't believe what I just read. I can't believe it."

Now that's Whoa, Wow, Hmmm, Yes.

You're impressed. Come on! You thought you knew everything about FedEx, but 'I've never seen that before'. Now, when you see a FedEx truck, if you've never seen the secret before, what are you going to notice?

This is a lean-forward-and-uncross-your-arms moment.

Let's look at other ways we can create those moments.

Storytelling. People remember stories. The reason the story works is, when you tell a story and you tell it sincerely, people lean in to identify with the characters. Tell a story that you're connected to, that's the key. You have to be connected to the story. Have characters people can relate to. Use stories which are relevant for the person that you're talking to. Here's an example. So, when I'm speaking with an educator at a university, I'll try to come up with stories about past experiences that were successful with other universities. If I'm relaying the success other universities have experienced with what I've sold them, that university wants to experience the same kind of success.

This creates a Whoa, Wow, Hmmm, Yes moment. People lean in and unfold their arms because you are relevant. When storytelling, be relevant, be clear, be concise, and be gone.

I have a feeling that you right now are listening for the 1116. It's a familiar number, but what was unfamiliar was the relationship between the numbers. Yes, you got it. 1116 stands for one day, one week, one month and six months. As a simple example, ask someone where they want to be in 1116. People will open, and the more they open, the more they will want to know what you have to say.

Here is a great example – 'I know what you are thinking right now, will you regret saying no if you don't buy, more than you will regret saying yes? Will you regret saying yes, in one day, one week, one month, and six months? Why would you regret it?' People will start to think of the situation differently. They may think, if I say yes, I may get in trouble. If I say no and the competitor buys, then the boss will ask, why didn't you buy?

Here is a story and an 'impossible' question I ask. I was on this television show called Review; I had written a book, but I wasn't a household name. And I remember the person connecting me up to the microphone, he was doing a good job and was really helpful. And I said, 'Can I ask you a question?' He looked at me fiercely because he thought I was going to ask for them to mention my book.

Instead, I asked, 'Let me ask you something: how long you been in this job?' He told me, five years. 'Where would you like to be in the job, in another five years?' And he says, 'I'd like to be an executive producer of a show like this'. So I used the impossible question, 'What would be an impossible thing for you to do to make this happen?' The man listed things he could do. And so, I said to him, 'Go do it!'

The man leaned in and said, 'I gotta tell you, I've been doing this for five years, and I've never had someone ask me such a helpful question'. And guess what, the man became a producer in under five years.

And we can do the same for our conversations with customers. What would be something that would be impossible for you to do, but if you could do, it would rapidly accelerate your success in your company? The customers lean in.

Every one of these questions and ideas I used during the pandemic, and engagement was incredible.

Here's another story and another Whoa, Wow, Hmmm, Yes question.

I remember my daughter, years ago, called me and she said, 'Dad, you're pretty good at this stuff. I'm going to be interviewing with someone from Lehman Brothers and it's not a formal interview, but you know, we're gonna have a conversation. And is there anything that I can ask him?'

I told her to ask the 'hypothetical' question and it went like this: "I have a hypothetical question. I'd like you to imagine. It's a year from now, and your boss says, 'the person you hired for the position, get us three more people like that, well done and you're getting a big raise.'" My daughter then asked, "What's the profile of the person you hire? What makes them so special?" He stopped, and replied, "That's a very good question, and I don't have an answer and I should'. She got the job.

I suggest using a hypothetical question with buyers. I'd like you to imagine at your next performance review and your boss is reviewing the marketing decisions you make, including buying ads. What would be the criteria for him to get a pay raise as a result?

Why this works is that you are not talking about business, you are talking about success and that has nothing to do with you making money.

Do you say that going to work every day is like winning the lottery? Do you feel like it's an honor and privilege? Is this what you tell family, friends, and strangers? If you don't, find a company where you do. Otherwise, you will never get customers leaning in.

Are you a noticer? Being a noticer is different than looking. It's called a beginner's mind. Make a point to notice something you've never noticed before, as if a blind person seeing it for the first time. Notice something in our customers that you never noticed before. Then we can work out how to respond to it, not just automatically responding."

- DR MARK GOULSTON

Mark is true to his purpose. In the two events we had with Mark, his humility won our hearts and minds – and those of Mrs. Leslie. He made us all very curious about what 1116 is! How will you feel in one day, one week, one month and six months from now, by saying NO. I have used this exercise favorably multiple times since the talk.

To end the session, Mark had us sing our troubles away. "It was ok," he told us, "you don't need to be a singer for this to work. It unblocks a closed mental state, and this is how you do it."

Remember a popular tune and then sing out loud, adding words to the tune about a topic you want to vent about and/or a negative emotion. Try it now! You may think it's crazy, but try it, it works – above all, it will make you smile. After the event we did a survey about this test and over 80% shared that it affected their state positively. Mark and I wrote a piece for Harvard Business Review on the tactic.

And finally, Mark shared a structure for giving a sincere thank you. Be specific, recognize the effort made and what it meant to you.

So, Mark, thank you for making the time to be a part of two ninety-minute calls to share your thoughts and tactics. We know that you are a busy man, and with time zones and your other engagements it took a lot to do this. This means so much to me, as I can align my values every day, and in learning new skills, I can achieve more of my outcomes in leaving people better than I find them.

Follow Mark at *markgoulston.com*

13

WHERE'S THE FOCUS?

APRIL 20, 2020

A conversation with
STEVE CLARKE

I LABELED THIS WEEK as 'British week'. Five of my mates from the British Isles were going to inspire us.

When I had my first ever speaking engagement in 2011, no one showed up. In the next room, Steve was talking and I sat and listened to him. He and I ended up becoming good friends.

Steve started off by saying we would have a conversation, not a presentation. His energy was contagious and he kept everyone engaged for well over an hour.

"I left school at sixteen, with no qualifications. I definitely didn't enjoy lessons, exam rooms, and the more formal side of education. By the time I was eighteen, I had gone through a number of dead-end jobs and found myself as a petrol pump attendant...

Then on a very stormy night this guy pulled up to the gas station in a beautiful MK4 Ford Cortina – at the time this was a top-of-the-range vehicle everyone wanted yet couldn't afford. When the guy asked me to fill up his car, I realized he was the same age as me.

I looked at him sitting inside of his car, out of the rain and in a smart suit. And there I was, soaking wet and filling up his car. It felt so wrong! I spoke to the guy and said, 'I hope you don't mind me asking, we are about the same age, what do you do for a living that gets you to wear a suit and drive this lovely car?'

He said to me, 'I am in sales'. He was a nice guy and handed me a cassette tape. He said, 'Listen to this, it helped me find my way and I am sure it will help you'.

When I got home, I listened to the cassette tape. What I heard was that, 'If you want to see a change, it's down to you,' and because of this I decided to change my life. I wanted to see change and I knew it was down to me to make it happen. That tape was Zig Ziglar, one of my personal favorites and one I've built my career on.

My journey in sales began. I learned quickly that the key to success in sales was, add value, build trust, and be nice. And be good at solving people's problems. Print those words out and put them on your wall! Nine months after starting in sales, I was the director of my first company at the tender age of nineteen.

That moment in the gas station and my experiences since then have meant I have been reasonably successful in business. I've started companies, I've floated one, I've sold a couple of other businesses. So, I've done reasonably well with what I've done in terms of growing, and scaling businesses, but not from having a business degree.

After a couple of years of success and when I sold my companies, I just didn't know what to do with myself because I had no purpose in my day. I had retired at forty-five and hadn't really thought about what retirement meant. I needed to find my why; what I was doing and why I was doing it - I needed some purpose in my day.

Simon's company Ink's product is travel which is one that people will want, not just need, your fortunes will return.

During the pandemic or in any given crisis, we can choose one of three options. You can hide, survive, or thrive, and there is no shame in whichever you choose right now.

Your attitude is the thing that will make you fly. It's all about what's in your mind. Sooner or later, the man who wins is the man who thinks he can. He read us this poem by Walter Wintle.

If you think you are beaten, you are;
If you think you dare not, you don't.
If you'd like to win, but you think you can't,
It is almost a cinch you won't.
If you think you'll lose, you've lost;
For out in this world we find
Success begins with a fellow's will
It's all in the state of mind.
If you think you're outclassed, you are;
You've got to think high to rise.
You've got to be sure of yourself before
You can ever win the prize.
Life's battles don't always go
To the stronger or faster man;
But sooner or later the person who wins
Is the one who thinks he can!

To prove it's all about attitude, I want you to play a word game. It's not all about hard work, it's not all about knowledge. It's about attitude. If we add up the number related to each letter in the alphabet a = 1, b = 2, c = 3 etc., then 'hard work' scores 98, 'knowledge' scores 96 – neither of these give 100. 'Ass-kissing' gives you 126 and 'Bullshit' 106.

'Attitude' scores 100, as it's the most important thing. Successful people have the attitude to take action and are action-oriented.

ATTITUDE is broken down like this:

Action (1)
Take responsibility (20)
Turn negatives into positives (20)
It takes excellence (9)
Turn your fear into focus (20)
Uncover hidden talents (21)
Develop yourself (4)
Expect the unexpected (5)

Winston Churchill had a great phrase when he talked about optimists and pessimists, it goes something like, An optimist sees the opportunity in every difficulty, and a pessimist sees the difficulty in every opportunity.

Do you have people around you who are fiercely negative? Find groups where you can get together and be positive around other people. If you sit around with negative people and if you watch the news morning, noon, and night, you will just drown in negativity. What we focus on is where your energy will go.

People want to hear from you. The law of reciprocity is so important right now, people will remember those who called just to see how things were.

One rule I have is, I call three people a day no matter what I am doing – friends, family. Who are those people you can call and help right now? In a sales environment, it's not just about calling people to sell stuff to. Who have you done business with in the past that you could call up and say thanks? Who could you call and just ask, how could you help them? People will remember you calling to check in. How could you help someone else without them asking?

During the day we all have an ultradian rhythm, a recurrent period or cycle repeated throughout a twenty-four-hour day. What happens is, if you sit at a desk, and work straight through and flat out all day, you'll just be exhausted. So, create what Steve calls 'Power Hour'; you work at your peak for the best part of forty-five minutes and then take fifteen minutes to get in the groove and rest. There are ups and downs, and you need to work in the peaks and rest in the troughs.

My family knows when my Power Hour is. A 'do not disturb' sign goes up on the door. During that time I need to be focused and concentrate. Knowing what I'm working on, clock starts, no distractions, no internet, no alerts coming up on my phone. I only work on things that will move me closer to my goals. I pick for my day the three things which will help me get to my goal quickest. I then focus on my monthly goals and then what I am looking to achieve yearly.

We need to plan individual and business plans every year – without one, we fail. We might have a plan when we start, and then we forget. I don't mean thirty pages of BS for the bank. I mean, a one page of where we are going, I call it a Sat Nav for business. What I mean by that is you wouldn't get in your car and drive from one city to another unless you absolutely knew the route.

Plan this – no complaining. You need seven consecutive days of no complaining. No complaining about anything, not about the kids, your partner, your work, college, the internet speed, the lack of toilet tissue, shops, whatever it is, for seven days there is to be no complaining about them. WHY? If you focus on the crap, guess what, you become a crap magnet, and no one likes a crap magnet because you're covered in that stuff, and you're not good to be around. When you focus on good stuff, more of the good stuff comes your way. People around you will see it, you attract more the right kind of people, and you'll be more fun to be around as well.

Is the coach or critic talking to you?

You need to tame those voices in your head, educate them and turn them into your coach, not your critic. If you're continually saying, 'Why does this always happen to me?' your subconscious will go and find all the reasons why this happens to you. The critic may say it's because you're useless, you're lazy, you're rubbish, you're ugly. You'll get some pretty shitty answers back because you are asking yourself critical questions and not coaching questions. Ask a coaching 'how' question. How can I get this done and have fun doing it? Then your mind starts to go off and find ways to get stuff done and have fun doing it.

Feel, felt, found – how do we use it in our sales story? I know how you feel, others felt just the same way. What they found was a Ziglar classic. Using this we sell with more compassion, and with more understanding for the fact that an awful lot of people are going through an awful lot of shit, financially, emotionally – you know, it's a bigger mess than people would have imagined. However, we will get through this."

- STEVE CLARKE

This was really powerful for me at the time, I thought I might have been in the hiding group that he mentioned. But Steve reminded us that our fortunes would be back soon enough. After this session as a group, we all encouraged our teams After this session as a group, we all encouraged our teams to do things no one could ever thank us for. We sent gifts, handwritten notes, we went above and beyond. We offered clients whatever help they needed. We offered to create messaging, write content, we offered to do it all for free. It was super powerful.

Since the pandemic began, Steve decided to stop doing the talks and focus on working with a few clients. You will find him on Facebook.

14

STORYTELLING IS THE KEY

APRIL 21, 2020

A conversation with
DARREN KELLY

I SPENT A LOT of time bitching on LinkedIn. One day I got a message from this chap, Darren Kelly, his outreach was great. I said call me, he did, and on that call I felt so engaged, I said I don't care what you are selling - I'm buying. He gave me some really useful advice. I invited him to chat about storytelling, outreach, and engaging prospective customers.

As a radio interviewer, Darren had the opportunity to interview many of the music greats, from George Michael to Cher, and his first message was to remember that they are just human like you and me. He asked us to understand things, to believe in them, and to remember them. The most important thing to do then is to take action.

Darren demonstrated in his event the power of storytelling; I am sure this was a lesson he learned from his time on the radio. With his stories and style, he helped us understand the many lessons he was sharing with us. It's all about storytelling.

> "There was a successful business leader from Indonesia, who during one financial turmoil lost absolutely everything. He had to take his family, wife, and children back to Indonesia as he had nothing. He was so embarrassed; he was depressed, and he just felt like giving up...
>
> His father said to him – wise man – think of the word 'gratitude'; gratitude is not just saying you're thankful for something, it's acting on that gratitude. One of the great things you can do when you feel helpless is define gratitude, he did, and started to do good things for other people. He didn't use gratitude just to feel good, he used it as a stepping stone, as his trampoline, as his setup for his comeback.
>
> Being alive today is enough to give us gratitude, especially in the current climate. But we must also have gratitude for our

talents and our skill sets. We're not just going to have gratitude and sit back, we're going to use gratitude as the foundation for creativity and as a foundation for hard work. Most people today are feeling sorry for themselves, and many businesses are giving up or shutting down, whereas if we apply gratitude, then the future is phenomenal.

The next story is about a man from Persia. He had this wonderful farm. One day, a man knocked on his door and said, there are diamonds around the world, and he could have some if he sold his farm and went looking. Well, he sold his farm, went off in search of diamonds, and he couldn't find any. The guy who bought the farm was walking on the farm one day and he saw something; he was standing on acres of diamonds. The original farmer killed himself because he was so depressed over the mistake he made. When you have an attitude of gratitude for your company, you'll find those acres of diamonds underneath.

This was a huge lesson, that where you are is sometimes the right place and you don't need to go off hunting elsewhere. I really wanted to drum this into my team during this period as many were starting to leave – I didn't blame them, but they were leaving behind acres of diamonds.

And what about customer gratitude?

Love your customer, it was something I learned in radio. My

customer was my listener and I knew that if I loved my listener, they would feel it when I was talking to them on air.

A great example of customer love: As Catholics, we weren't allowed to eat meat on Fridays. In America, McDonald's realized this problem, and one of their franchisees in Cincinnati, which has a large population of Catholics, put catfish on the menu on Fridays, and you can imagine the results. What an example of customer gratitude, adapting to what your prospective customers and clients really need, and adding value.

An example of a great salesperson, look no further than Charles Dickens. To begin with he was one of the first people to put adverts in his books! Dickens showed his understanding of sales in A Christmas Carol. Think about the characters – Scrooge is like your client, many of them are stuck in a mindset and they don't want to change. So, Dickens had an idea on how to change that mindset. He sent in a ghost called Marley, he was basically the marketing guy. And then after that, he sent in three salespeople: the Ghosts of Christmas Past, Present, and Future. What do they do? They showed Scrooge the pain in his past, the pain in his present, and what he was going to face in the future, if he didn't change. And what happened at the end? Scrooge changed his life, he ran down the street faster than Usain Bolt full of Christmas love.

Okay, so I am sure you have worked out what this means to salespeople; we must understand our customers' past because their past will dictate the decisions that they make. Understand their current pain and show them where their future is going to be. Then offer a solution.

Love is the answer

Did you know love comes from preparation? Imagine if you are going to make a marriage proposal to someone, and if you have to wonder if the person is going to say yes, then obviously you don't know the person well enough. Poor preparation! If you give off a love that is so infectious because you have prepared, you bring value to the table that they understand. You're bringing value, you are there as a servant. An attitude of I'm going to serve these people, I love them, I want them to do well, and I want the customer to grow their business. I want the person who's going to make this decision to feel good, I want them to feel that they've not just got a partner in growth, they've got a friend, and someone they can rely on. If you have that attitude, it's infectious.

If during this process you sound nervous, think of Frank Sinatra. After all, a client can hear you sounding stressed and nervous, and if they do, they lose confidence. So here's the Frank technique to controlling stress and nerves. It's a simple strategy of breathing – there were many great singers around during Frank's time but no one as good as him. Why? He was the only one who practiced his breathing. My technique is the

4-7-8 breathing technique, also known as 'relaxing breath', involves breathing in for 4 seconds, holding the breath for 7 seconds, and exhaling for 8 seconds. This breathing pattern aims to reduce anxiety.

And what about the words you use? Get rid of the clichés and don't use words that people don't understand. Stop trying to impress your listener, he was told once. Instead, express what you feel. Stop trying to sound more intellectual, stop using jargon that the customers don't understand, and lose the ego. Make sure that the language you use is simple.

Talking too fast – it happens to us all when we are so excited about what we have to say that we never slow down. This means we can sometimes hate and be afraid of silence. Silence is powerful. Be aware that what we think is a long silence is not a long silence for someone who's listening to you on the phone. The greatest radio broadcasters from around the world, the greatest salespeople, know how to use the power of the silence.

I am sure at times you will all face being brushed off on the phone. Even during radio interviews people were rude. You need to have a forgiving nature. So if I'm in an interview with someone, I never label them rude or bad. I think we're human beings and we all make mistakes, and I like to give people the benefit of the doubt. So, if someone's being rude to me, I developed in my own mindset, and internally said, That's fine, you're having a bad day, but you ain't going to impact me. People just want to vent and perhaps you're the only one prepared to listen. It's not personal.

The superstar Ricky Martin, he was late for the interview, walked in with five different bodyguards and had a very stormy face and manner. The first thing I said to him was, 'Ricky, before we do the interview, can I just say that I love the work you do with the Ricky Martin Foundation'. His eyes lit up and he was the nicest guy. He even went around the whole building, taking pictures with all the girls and boys. Never judge anyone.

What do you do when you face challenges?

Try my 'Hello Technique'; it stands for:

- **HONOR THE FACTS**. Don't exaggerate your problems, we all have a tendency to do this. Too many people put their problems away. It's about getting to the root of the problem. How big a problem is it? How fast can you solve it? What is the truth about it? Is it hearsay from someone else, is it gossip? How can I verify these facts?
- **ENGAGE SUPPORT**. You've got to make sure that you engage support. See everything from every single angle and ask who can help? If you can't do it yourself, get someone to help you.

- **LEVERAGE THAT SUPPORT.** How can you utilize the support you have engaged? Tap into the resources.
- **LEAD TO ACTION.** There is no point getting all these insights and support if you don't take action.
- **OPTIMIZE THE OUTCOME.** The outcome might be a negative outcome or a positive outcome. How do we optimize the negative outcome? I'll give you a simple example, 'When something bad happens, or something doesn't go right. Always ask yourself, what is this experience teaching me? What have I learned from it? How can I use it going forward? How can I help someone else with this going forward?"

- DARREN KELLY

A great example of storytelling and the power of tonality and passion. After all, who fails to hear when passion speaks? If the person we are talking to on the radio, the phone, or face to face, feels our love, then we are connected. Throw in a splash of value, then we make a sale. When we are talking to our customers, they can feel it if you really care for them, they can feel it if you prepare, and they can feel it if you can see things from their side of the argument.

Darren can be found at *thesalesiq.com*

15

THE ENERGY IN THE ROOM

APRIL 22, 2020

A conversation with
JAMES HARRIS

DAY THREE OF BRITISH WEEK and I found a force like no other. This guy boomed into our Zoom room. It was early in LA and of all the speakers this man's energy was off the Richter scale. James was from London and had worked around the corner from our office, yet today he was a TV star and property sales guru.

One of my colleagues reached out to him and he graciously offered to help, and help he did. British charm and style with American energy, that's how James has been described. After he decided that he was bored of the cold weather, he moved to LA for the land of sun and opportunity, and the rest is legend. He has since become famous for his lead in the US TV show Million Dollar Listing: LA. This event was indeed a masterclass in selling, not just theoretical, but practical from a person who has been where we are, learned along the way, and now is enjoying the benefits of his hard work.

> "False evidence appearing real – that's what fear is. I've learned that fear and faith cannot coexist. To diminish fear, make it small so that it becomes nonexistent. If it jumps up in front of you, squash it...

You have to carry a positive mentality – you show up like you're ready to be successful. A way of doing this is to structure your day. Even during the pandemic, I structured my day. I had the same routine as pre-pandemic. Up at six, running by six thirty, having breakfast by eight thirty, and I'm in my office by nine. I've showered, done my hair, put on my cologne, and dressed for success. My thinking is really simple – if I feel good then I can send that message out there, and that's what I expect to get back. Put out what you want to get back.

At times, staying positive was difficult. At the start of the pandemic I was glued to CNN; I was glued to my Facebook feed, and I was terrified. It was difficult not to live in fear. So, I advise you to avoid those negative influences. The fact is you don't need to watch the news, just talking to people you get a sense of what's going on. I knew that if things changed and got bad, at least twenty-five people would reach out and tell me what was happening because people love to live in fear.

What are the negative things you are listening to each day to stop you being positive? Remove yourself from them.

And it's the same when selling on the phone; you may change your pitch for what you're selling, but the energy has to remain the same. You have to be positive. You have to enjoy what you're doing; you have to have excitement about it, you have to believe in it. This attitude needs to be in every call and people will remember you. They will know you to have a positive energy. This is what separates me and you from the next person. The second that they hear my voice, I sound more excited, more energetic, and more powerful than the person that called them before. You have to get that excitement going from the second they answer the phone.

Always ask for the money, and don't be afraid of the price. You may not be able to afford the product you are selling, that doesn't mean that the person on the other end of the phone cannot. You have to lose the fear, never let that fear get in the way of asking for big money. The only difference between a thousand-dollar deal and a five-hundred-thousand-dollar one is your pay cheque, and that increases by five hundred times. Since the pandemic, our average deal size grew from about five thousand dollars to over fifty thousand dollars – I wonder if this helped our thinking, too.

Create value and that's not just based on features and benefits; be creative and think outside of the box, show them something that they wouldn't ordinarily see in the normal way they would have seen it. Craft your pitch so it's unique to you, not imitating what the person next to you is doing is doing. A great way to understand your value is by asking my favorite question to the buyer: 'Why work with me?' The buyer then sells themselves back to you.

Learn your market and educate, because information is key. If I drive to Bel Air today, I know every single house, I know what it's sold for, I know what it's traded for two times before I know which agents are there, I know who owns it. I know what houses are coming up, what houses have sold, and I believe you need to learn your market inside out, back to front, if you're going to truly succeed.

When I started in the real estate business, I could not tell you the way from my house to Beverly Hills, which was three minutes away. One of my first clients, a lady called Janice, wanted to see ten houses back-to-back, and she wanted to follow me between houses. I was so nervous and anxious that I was a sweating mess, it was just uncomfortable. Funny thing, after the viewings she said she had lived in LA her whole life and didn't know all those back streets. The moral of the story is, unless you are fully prepared, you cannot demonstrate your value and show where your value lies.

How do you deal with 'no', James?

We have all heard this one, every time you hear the word 'no', you're closer to a 'yes' – it's mindset, it's mentality, it's energy. If your mindset is on a failure, that you can't succeed, and how are you going to get to the next deal? Then the chances are you're not going to get to the next deal. If you have a positive mindset and positive energy, you will think that every time you hear that word 'no', you are closer to a 'yes', and you will be.

Instead of dialing a hundred people a day, dial a hundred-and-fifty people a day. It's a numbers game, it's your responsibility to turn them into a yes. With positive energy, keep going, stay focused. Raise the numbers and you'll raise the paycheck, guaranteed.

Smiling and dialing – I love this, when I get bored and frustrated, I sit up and work on my posture, this makes it easier to smile. When you're smiling it creates positive energy, and guess what, it's contagious.

Closing, you need to visualize the close, *see it* and *feel it*. You need to believe in yourself and live on the side of faith and not fear. Here is one of my favorites:

The takeaway close. If you give something to someone and then you take it away and they can't have it, they want it ten times more. I had two people interested in the same house. Both are pitching me they like the property. I'm pitching them that I completely understand that they like this house. One hadn't viewed the property, so I told them, 'I cannot sell you this house because you haven't seen it, and I have a local buyer who has seen the house' The buyer flew in the next day, and I had the house tied up in escrow for five-hundred-thousand dollars higher than what I had from the other local people. Every single client is very different. One client may turn around and say 'Well, fuck it, I don't need it anyway'. You've got to know who you're dealing with. You have to be able to tell if that client needs to have a hardcore pitch or if that client needs to feel like they're controlling you.

I'm the CEO of my own business, you're your own boss, you write your own paychecks, right? So, if I'm dealing with a lead that feels like it's hot and I feel like I'm going to close it, I'll spend as long as I need on closing it. But not if I feel for one minute that I'm dealing with a buyer that's not real, that doesn't have the money, that's wasting my time. You need to understand who's real and who's not, as early as you can.

You have to provide the value, that's how you become the master of your craft. You have to art and craft your deals. Always start with the bigger number, and let people negotiate themselves down, versus programming their minds with a lower number, and then having to get them up.

You need to be a deal junkie, excited about what you do, even if you're selling the same thing over and over again. Every deal is different because you're dealing with somebody different, and the way the deal goes down is different, and you have to make it fun for yourself. Every deal I do, I'm buzzing about closing. Once it closes, my team take over and I'm onto the next. The harder or more complex the sale, the more I get excited I get to make it happen.

Then you can move on to the next – You're only as good as your next deal. It's important to get back on the phone immediately and make the next call. The vast majority of people put the phone down, celebrate, and become complacent and lazy. Don't do it – that's the time to pound the phones, that's the time to pick up the phone and make a hundred phone calls. I always say that's when you have money in your voice."

- JAMES HARRIS

As James wrapped up the questions, we were buzzing with energy, and we asked him how he had so much energy. He said, "Look, I don't consider this as work, I want to give out what I want to get back." He finished by saying that having energized us, he was going to have a better day because of this. Start your day positive, keep your energy high, work out, manifest, and believe. James said a huge thank you to those in Singapore who stayed up late to listen, as that demonstrated huge belief in the business and what we do. He said it showed dedication and care.

And OMG, James was full of energy during this event – I think if I showed up today and I was negative, down, and I didn't have that energy, I don't think this call would have been successful and I don't think everyone would have walked away with as much positive information.

My fear during the current pandemic could be that people will not buy, so what's going to happen? I had to change my thinking to the fact that people have more money now than they've ever had before, that they're ready to start buying right now, and I should be calling them to explain why.

Every time I felt a little low during the pandemic, I watched James' talk again.

James can be found on Instagram *@jamesbondst*

16

HAVE FAITH IN YOURSELF

APRIL 23, 2020

A conversation with
DREWE BROUGHTON

I REACHED OUT to Drewe having seen his content on social media. He helps people deal with fear and stress. As an ex-professional footballer, he was not someone I thought would have suffered so much. He offered an alternative view to many things. He started by showing a video of the highs and lowlights of his life.

Drewe shared his personal journey with honesty about the emotional pressure he faced when on the spot, taking a penalty. It's a story of overcoming the negative voices, the negative external criticism, and to use second-half thinking.

"Sometimes we don't think of the pressure of performance that athletes have. Thousands of people, expecting you to perform in that moment, and you only have ninety minutes to be your best – and in many cases, a few minutes to secure your place on the pitch...

Keep it simple and don't over-complicate life. We live in a world full of data, analysis and advice. What we need to do is listen to our instincts, not the data. It's all about the stats for the best players in the world. You're always competing against those numbers. I was paid to score goals. At the top end of the pitch, where you're paid the most, it's the biggest pressure. Don't let the data stop you, focus on the right things, and again, listen to your instincts.

Each time you play in that hour and a half, you are playing for, or to keep, your contract. I remember a particular time when in the first half of a game everything was going wrong with my performance. In fact, I was told by the manager at halftime, I would play for another ten more minutes, and then I was off the pitch. If that happened, the reality of the situation was I would have left the stadium and been out of work with no way of paying the bills. I just had to make the second half work. And I did, relying on instinct and practicing what I call the 'overview effect'. This is when astronauts go to space, then they come back and report a complete shift in consciousness and awareness. When viewing Earth from space, they start to realize the complete lack of power we have as humans. And for me, this realization meant the recognition that it was my ego driving my poor performance. Only when I listened to my instincts did I change my second-half performance.

As quickly as the success comes, it goes. For six months I slept in my car. My marriage was finished, I wasn't able to see my child and possibly never get the chance to be a good father. My finances were crap and I owed about seventy-five thousand pounds on my credit cards. I reflected on my life and found a sense of peace through surrender.

Being brutally honest, I find myself. There was no one adding anything to me. So, I lifted, brick by brick, all the debris that had me buried in that moment. I had to remember that talented boy who was good at school, the center of jokes at parties, the good guy, and the well-thought-of and well-brought-up guy. It was a spiritual experience; I just think there's such a fine line between spirituality, emotions, feelings, religion. I completely believe in spiritual sense. I don't believe anybody can fulfill their potential, unless they tap into the spiritual realm. We're all going to have to tap into a source greater. You have to have courage to be you. Feel it. Feel everything you need to feel. Don't care what anyone else thinks about you.

So, what can football teach us about sales?

Salespeople are like strikers; if they're not selling every day, they're miserable. Don't overthink everything. In a moment of pressure, like when taking a penalty, be in the moment. You cannot agree in advance the names of the players who are going to take the penalty as it doesn't account for pressure and fatigue. You got to ask people in the moment and ignore the critics. When I volunteered to take the penalty, no one else volunteered. I was a substitute who came on for the last twenty-five minutes. I was not one of the players who was respected at that time. I ignored everything, applied my overview effect, and followed my instincts. And I scored.

Some of my coaching experiences has been with golfers. Ignore the stats and get back to enjoying what you do. When you were relaxed and playing your best, what did you do? If it was eating a chocolate bar or drinking coke before you played, then do it. Get back in touch with who you were. Go out there, take a deep breath, don't block those emotions, if we block that closes our creativity. What would the child in you do? We do need to think and behave like children, go back to a time when anything was possible.

When it's tough, remind yourself of your goals and vision. In those tough times, ask yourself: what do you see in yourself? What do you want? What are you capable of? Remind yourself of these things to keep you going when it's tough. You are unbelievable. And you don't realize just how good you are and how good you can be.

Understanding yourself with honesty, authenticity, and having an overview is the place where performance starts. You are only as good as the way you are playing in that moment, and use this as a motivation to perform without forgetting to keep it simple and go with your instinct."

- DREWE BROUGHTON

Drewe is *@the_fear_coach* on Instagram

17

UNDERSTANDING THE BRAIN

APRIL 24, 2020

A conversation with
SIMON HAZELDINE

FINAL TALK OF BRITISH WEEK came from a man who knows more about what's going through our heads than we do. What does an ex-bouncer and bodyguard know about sales, negotiation, business performance, and applied neuroscience? The answer is loads – so welcome to Simon Hazeldine.

> "How successfully do you differentiate your company from your competitors?...

Get out your own heads, get inside your customers' heads; for too many salespeople it's one-way traffic, it's about them. Customers do not care about you. They don't care about your organization; they don't care about your products. They don't care about your offices. They don't care about your awards, all they care about is how you can help them to get what they want.

Show how you can help them get what they want, and they'll buy from you. Tell stories because people listen to a story, they identify with the story, and they put themselves in the story. Computer scientists had people in fMRI (functional magnetic resonance imaging) scanners, which monitor blood flow and show which parts of the brain are reactive to a story. The emotional center of the brain is activated when people are listening. When we tell stories, we are implanting thoughts and ideas and emotions into the brains of our listeners.

GET OUT OF YOUR OWN HEAD. GET INSIDE YOUR CUSTOMER'S HEAD. ALWAYS THINK, CUSTOMER FIRST.

Don't fight reality, because reality will win. We cannot control what's happening, but we can control how we react. And it's down to three things: Mindset, skillset and toolset.

It's really about these three things – how we think about things, how good we are at handling the situation, and what software we have to make our lives easier. If we can conquer these three things, we will become hugely successful.

ALL THE BILLIONAIRES I'VE MET ARE POSSIBILITY THINKERS. THEY THINK MOST THINGS ARE POSSIBLE.

As we come out of this season, we need to be match-fit and ready to fight again. We will need vibrant companies to pay for the cost of this pandemic. It's so important for the economy to rebound. Make sure you are ready for the rebound. We need to be better at understanding our customers' needs.

Storytelling is the only way, and the way to structure a story is to imagine a house – and draw it. I call it the 'message house'.

- **The roof of the house is your main message, that's the thing you most want people to remember.**
- **Then three pillars support it. Those are your three key points that support your main message.**
- **And in the basement, the foundations are your fact foundation.**

Example – your main message, 'we believe we're the best partner,' or 'we believe this is the right thing for you because...' These are the three most important things - one, two, three. Finally, 'Here's the proof we've done it for someone else', and have case studies and testimonials.

Have a look at your sales proposals and count how many times you mentioned your company, how many times you mentioned the customer. Make sure it's customer-focused; customer first, that's what creates differentiation.

The brain remembers primacy, and recency. It remembers the first thing you say, and it remembers the last thing it hears. After the little bit of preamble, open with a statement or a question that really gets people hooked, gets people thinking. And then finish strongly with a powerful value statement.

Give things in threes. Threes are very memorable as the brain remembers by linkage. It also remembers enthusiasm, and anything unusual or different. Do they want to survive, then to strive, and then, finally, to prosper?

That's why David Meltzer talks in threes.

Ask really good questions to really understand what the customer needs. What is the customer's situation? What problems are they experiencing? Then dig deeper – what is the impact of that problem if that problem is not solved? What is the impact if you could help them get the results they're looking for? Moving away from problems, moving away from pain is more of a powerful motivator for most human beings than moving towards pleasure. Questioning based on the impact of that problem will really motivate, and when you show them the solution, they will listen.

We have to get to understand people's level of risk when making a buying decision. Buying a coke from the store is a minimal risk because it's a low price, it's a known brand, and if you get it wrong, it doesn't really matter. But the higher the level of revenue or the more unusual the purchase, the higher the potential risk perception. You have to make it seem as safe as possible. Keep that emotional part of the brain feeling comfortable and show low risk by giving examples and case studies of others.

The most powerful thing in the psychology of persuasion is social proof. Human beings are very influenced by other human beings, particularly if they're feeling uncertain. Amazon is a great example of this. Five star reviews are social proof; 95% of people looked at this book, bought this book, 5% bought something else and then 67% of people who bought this also bought this. It's all about social proof.

Connect at a human level. Build a different kind of relationship by connecting on an emotional level. This superior connecting and interacting with our customers on an emotional level is very important.

We are all largely emotional creatures. I think empathy is critically important. I would draw a distinction between empathy and sympathy. Empathy is an understanding of how somebody is feeling and showing your sensitivity towards that, whereas with sympathy, you may start to experience the same emotion that that person is having.

I see two broad mindsets that people have: 'probability thinking' – which is fixed – and 'possibility thinking' – only limited by the laws of gravity. There is a now-famous prediction from an IBM president in 1950, who thought there was a worldwide market for only five computers. They had a very fixed view of what's likely to happen. Jeff Bezos believes he is only limited by the laws of physics. So, if it isn't a law of physics, he thinks there must be some way, some possibility.

We can't control our customers, but we can influence our customers. What we can control, for example, is the number of calls we make, the duration of those calls and their quality. First and foremost, focus on things you can control.

- **SPHERE OF CONTROL** – things over which we have the final say, we determine the outcome. For example, 'My email inbox has 562 unread messages in it, and I am so stressed out'. Number of calls; Quality of calls.
- **SPHERE OF INFLUENCE** – issues that we can influence, although we alone do not determine the outcome. Such as, 'My assistant works so slowly, it's easier if I just do it myself – but that means working longer hours'.
- **SPHERE OF NO CONTROL/NO INFLUENCE** – matters that are out of our control or beyond our influence. For example, 'My job requires heavy travel and I never get to see my family'.

We must stay in an 'optimum state of arousal' – don't get too excited. It's not nearly as interesting as some of you are now thinking. In sports, this is about changing our mood and how we are thinking and feeling. Ways of doing this can include making sure you get a lot of breaks; your physiology affects your mental state.

What are you focusing on inside, the pictures you're making and the words you are using? Positive mantras – it's not mystical woo-woo. But athletes using mantras like 'faster, faster, faster' have better results. Using mental visualization – so before you pick up the phone or go into a meeting with a customer, visualize the outcome you want - what I want the customer to be thinking, saying, doing, or feeling at the end of this call - then work backwards from that.

Did you know 99.7% of gold-medal-winning Olympic athletes report using mental rehearsal and imagery. So, they visualize and imagine in their mind, not only the outcomes they want to have, but also strategies for problem-solving, like getting boxed into the wrong lane. They mentally plan and mentally rehearse, and self-talk. Stand up, get moving, or watch something funny for twenty, thirty minutes. Do something for someone else; a planned or random act of kindness, maybe just reach out to someone and say 'hi.' Or, when you're in the supermarket getting your groceries, say 'thanks very much' to staff, have a little conversation, or go check on one of your neighbors.

By the way, in the brain, when you do things for other people – kindness, altruism – you get a chemical kick back, so the brain rewards you for being kind to other people, it makes you feel good.

STOP

Imagine you're fighting your enemy in a sword battle. Your focus is on the here and now, on survival; you've got a very narrow perspective. In terms of neuroscience, this is the connection I made; the emotional area of the brain is more aroused and is more active, and when the emotional region of the brain is particularly active, the rational part does not work as effectively. If you stepped out of that battle, and you went up the valley side, your perspective would change. You'd move away from the here and now, the rush, the incoming fighting, and you'd be able to see a little bit further and your brain literally calms down. What it actually does, from a neuroscience point of view, is it helps to activate that prefrontal cortex, which allows you to think more rationally, or more altogether.

Remember, S. T. O. P: Step back, Think, Organize, Proceed back down."

- SIMON HAZELDINE

75% of us thought we were doing a good job at standing apart from our competitors, when Simon asked the question.

He went on to say, "When I talk to customers and ask, 'What percentage of salespeople that you see successfully differentiate themselves from the competition?', they say 3%!"

So, what can we do to differentiate from our competitors?

We all have a constructed image of ourselves that we've built up over time. It's referred to as your self-image – that is, the image you have of yourself. It's accurate, sometimes, but really, it's all inaccurate. So have a realistic assessment of where we're strong, have a realistic understanding of where we're not so great. Sometimes we are tougher on ourselves than we are on other people.

You can reach Simon at *simonhazeldine.com*

18

BREATHING LIFE BACK INTO YOU

APRIL 27, 2020

A conversation with
WIM HOF

I WAS ASKED, "Can you get Wim Hof?" I said, "I can get anybody." With a little help from my Swedish colleague, we got The Iceman to join us late in April. It was a wonderful learning moment.

Crazy or superman? He has been considered both. He is known as "The Iceman" because he broke so many records related to cold exposure – climbing Mount Kilimanjaro in shorts, running a half-marathon above the arctic circle on his bare feet, and standing in a container while covered with ice cubes for more than twelve minutes.

Wim told us he "started forty-three years ago." He began off by telling us to get high off our own supply.

"You are stronger than you think you are! Over time, we have disconnected with nature. And this has meant we have lost the ability to tap into our inner power. I reconnect us with that inner power...

I believe that we have so much more control, and potential than we realize. And for twenty-five years, I was doing my practices, completely alone, like a monk. And then, somebody told the television, 'there is a man, he goes underneath the ice, and he disappears and five minutes later, he comes back; he looks like a human, and behaves like a seal'. Then I got the interest of the scientists, they saw me doing 'scientifically impossible' things. Our bodies have an absolute greater power than we think, or normally test, to adapt to the elements of nature to stress.

So, how did I do it? I built it up, and I learned to feel. Toughness leads to control. It's pure control. This is what I've been showing in brain scans at the University of Michigan. They pour ice water on the skin, and just by the control of the mind, I was able to make the skin temperature not go down. It's the real power of the mind separate from the body. It's there, and we need to learn to control and take it.

Breathing gives us potential, and as silly as that statement seems, we don't use it to its potential. Heightened oxygen levels give us more energy, reduce stress levels, and enhance our immune system.

Sit in a comfortable position – without restricting the movement of your lungs.

Close your eyes, clear your mind.

Inhale deeply through the nose or mouth, and exhale unforced through the mouth.

Fully inhale through the belly, then chest and then let them go unforced.

Repeat these thirty to forty times in short, powerful bursts.

After the last exhale, inhale one final time as deeply as you can.

Then let the air out and stop breathing. Hold until you feel the urge to breathe again.

Then take time to bask in the bliss.

The second way we can connect with our inner power is by cold therapy – this is about being an alchemist. We need to expose ourselves to the cold, as the health benefits are huge. Wim says it balances hormone levels, improves sleep, produces endorphins (which elevates mood), fortifies immune systems, and speeds up metabolisms. Another benefit of exposing your body to cold is that it reduces inflammation, swelling, and sore muscles. Exposure to cold

> speeds up recovery after physical exercise.
>
> So, take an ice bath or shower. Start with a one-minute immersion once a week. When the cold hits you, keep breathing long, deep breaths through the cold. And then you will find that your muscle tension goes down, and you are in control."
>
> **- WIM HOF**

Wim's stories left us energized; this man had gone from being ridiculed to being a genius and we were graced to learn so much from him; he spent nearly two hours with our team. During the last year every morning, until things got better, I did the breathing exercises as I woke up (I wonder why I stopped?) and I tested cold showers, went back to cryotherapy, and swam in the cold British sea.

He taught us a breathing technique – he said we should do this before each phone call to get in the right state of mind. It takes two minutes, and afterwards you feel fully charged, relaxed and not anxious or stressed. You will have manipulated the chemistry in the body.

We learned many exercises which are on his free app at *wimhofmethod.com*

19

EVERYBODY NEEDS
A COACH

APRIL 30, 2020

A conversation with
COACH MICHEAL BURT

I MET COACH BURT a few years earlier, but he didn't remember me when I called and asked him to come and chat to the team. He agreed with pleasure, and during the last eighteen months Micheal and I worked closely together and became good pals. I am grateful for his support. He worked with my Miami team to show them resilience during the pandemic and I believe some of their strength came from that coaching. His tagline is 'everybody needs a coach in life'. I needed him during this time.

"Being a high school basketball coach for fourteen years prepared me for the demands of adult and business coaching, or so I thought. Coaching high school was a lot easier...

I was tough and disciplined with those high school basketball players, and they were tough as well. But when coaching adults, they weren't even close to the work of high school kids. I had to change my approach, I had to soften up for adults because they weren't tough enough, they would break down and start crying. They wanted to quit when you gave them negative feedback; you couldn't be critical of them and only a few of them wanted to go to the next level.

I couldn't understand this. I was raised by a single mother who had me when she was sixteen years old in a small town in Tennessee. And she was tough. She wouldn't let me miss a day of school. Her philosophy was, 'When you know you're going to show up, you are going to grow up and you are going to deliver'. She said: **'We don't want, we don't mind, and we don't make any excuses'**.

My main attitude is, *Will I be better today than I was yesterday, will I be better tomorrow than I was today?* It's about never stopping getting better, unless we choose to stop. Many people, unfortunately due to a lack of confidence, choose to stop getting better. It's all about confidence, I want you to think about confidence as a science. Confidence is not arrogance. Arrogance is when your self-appraisal is much higher than your market value. In essence, you're really not that good, you just think you're that good. Lots of people become successful and they become arrogant. You can't be successful without all the answers, but work hard to find them, always be open to anything, closed off to nothing. I never want to come across as arrogant, although some insecure people see confident people as arrogant.

Losing confidence happens to us all. At twenty-five years old, I lost every bit of my confidence. I was clinically depressed for six months, couldn't get out of bed, couldn't eat. I thought depression was a weakness. I thought people who got depressed were weak. And then I personally experienced that depression. I had to fight my way out of it. I started studying confidence. I made up my mind that nothing external would ever control my confidence for the rest of my life. I would never put my confidence in the hands of another person. I would always put my destiny in my own hands. I bounced back and I have lived to that over the last eighteen years of my life. I diversify my confidence, meaning I don't put all of my confidence in one thing. Make sure you have more than one stream to focus on, to build your confidence. I build confidence in my body, mind, spirit, and emotion, and then I feed that confidence daily. Don't make the mistake of getting and relying on one area to give you confidence.

CONFIDENCE IS THE MEMORY OF SUCCESS.

When I'm feeling low in confidence, I go back to a moment in life when I was incredibly successful. The night I won a championship as a basketball coach. Ten thousand people were cheering for me and the team, and I was standing in the middle of it. I say to myself, 'You're not an insecure person. Look at what you did, you won a championship, you built a multimillion-dollar company, you've raised an incredible daughter'.

YOU BUILD CONFIDENCE THROUGH REPETITION.

I used to make my basketball players shoot five hundred free practice. With muscle memory and repetition, you become great. The military trains every day and world class Olympians train every day. Successful people train every day. Unsuccessful people train every now and then. Mastery takes ten-thousand hours of training, that's how you master something. Ask yourself: Do you want to go pro or do you want to remain an amateur? Because pros spend time in preparation. I spend two to four hours every week, just planning. Amateurs roll into the week, no plan, no strategy, they haven't sourced any leads, they don't have a hit list. Then it takes them till Wednesday to get cranked up, and they've wasted half the week. Remember that progress is just as important as perfection, as long as we're making progress every day. You need to get out of the perfectionism trap, perfectionism leads to procrastination. Be interested in progress versus perfection.

Repetition and daily habits build confidence. Here's my daily routine; I wake up in the morning, first thing I do is change my state. I listen to something spiritual. Then, I exercise at a pretty high pace. I listen to something on business as I'm getting ready and I'm fixing my hair! I spend a little bit of time with my wife and my daughter. And all of this is achieved before 0700. I get into the office by 0800, having fed my mind, body, heart, and spirit. Guess what, my confidence is high.

I probably practiced my presentations a hundred times before I got on stage; the rhythm, the cadence, the movement – it's proactive and repetitive. When you're prepared you feel confident, and through execution, you feel confident.

Here are some of the things we can do:

- Have the mindset: go to bed tired and wake up hungry.
- Have the attitude that it all goes to zero at midnight.

I often say to salespeople who are selling to me, 'You don't even believe in your product or service. You cannot sell without conviction. You're not selling a product or service, you're selling a conviction, you're selling a set of beliefs; you're selling that you're going to be better off with me in your life than you are with somebody else in your life. You're selling an outcome.

Confidence helps us understand that there is no wasted engagement because we don't know where the next big deal is going to come from. I did a workshop one night, and two people showed, each paid $40. Rather than canceling, I didn't. Had no idea one of those people was a CEO for a fifty-million-dollar company, who came up to me afterward and said, 'You're exactly what we've been looking for. They signed up for a four-year deal and it's one of my largest contracts.

But I also had a presentation when everything went wrong. I couldn't get in a rhythm. We didn't sell anything, no shirts or books, and I left that weekend thinking, *Oh my gosh, I was so bad*. The following week I got a call from someone who had seen me at the presentations, and they said, 'We love you', and signed up for $350,000 of coaching. Why, when I was so bad, did they buy? The answer was, I showed up, and I had enough conviction to overcome how bad I was that day. The reality is, if you uncover enough rocks, if you talk to enough people, and if you keep showing up, other people will be inspired by what you're doing, and other people want to move towards you.

So, when you think about confidence and someone performing at their maximum potential in body, mind and spirit, they are totally independent of the opinions of others. Meaning they cannot control your confidence. No external factor can control your confidence. For example, politics, the economy and the government can't control you.

Sometimes, our confidence gets beaten down, and because of it we start making concessions. We lose confidence in what we are selling. We question whether maybe we should discount our services; maybe they can't afford it, or maybe they can't do it! When I was at an airport once, it was a lesson, an example of concession and pitiful thinking. A man came up to me, he looked rough, incredibly rough, like he hadn't slept in days, and with a look like life had beaten him up and he said, 'Coach I want to buy copies of your book for every one of my employees', and the first words out of my mouth were, 'I can't give you a discount'. He turned out to be a multimillionaire, and I had made a judgment that he didn't have any money; the first words out of my mouth were 'I can't give you a discount on the book'. He said, 'I didn't ask you for a discount!'

You need to remove all those internal thoughts that prohibit an action, and until you remove them, you will never reach your full potential. If you gave me the number of any person on planet Earth today, I would call them with no hesitation whatsoever. I don't care how much money they have, I don't care where they come from, I don't care what they've done in their life.

The money will follow you all the way to the bank. When problems are solved, the bigger the problem, the more money people pay to solve that problem. You don't just get paid in money; money is a byproduct of value creation. When you distribute your talent to the world, the world rewards you. Think of athletes, artists, and entertainers; if you've ever gone to a concert and paid money to watch an entertainer perform, you are paying to watch them work. If you distribute your talents to the world at a very high frequency, you will make a lot of money because money follows excellence, money follows action, and money follows movement. Nothing happens until something is sold. So, focus on building long-term wealth through your sales ability.

The final thought is about the 'prey drive'. This is one of my signature pieces. You need to understand what your prey drive is. The dictionary definition is the instinctive inclination of a carnivore to find, pursue, and capture prey. It's about capturing and getting what you want.

Competition activates prey drive. Fear of loss activates prey drive. Use that fear as fuel.

- COACH MICHEAL BURT

Coach told us his "number one motivator is a fear of loss environment." He wakes every day, scared that he is going to lose everything.

Exposure. Once you get exposed to a better way you never go back to your original dimension. Embarrassment, and I don't embarrass people if they're not performing at the level they're capable of. The most common prey drive for top performers is typically stimulated by competition, or fear of loss.

Focus on building long-term wealth. Money doesn't buy you freedom, skills buy you freedom. The stronger your skill is, the more money you're going to make. The energy in the session was high throughout and the guys asked some great questions. We were ending April in a good mood, after thirteen wonderful talks, great messages, and connections with some of the most powerful and inspirational speakers on the planet.

We were sure he also referenced Game of Thrones – he told us, "Winter is coming! We need to ask ourselves when winter comes, what did we do all spring and summer? 'Winter Is coming', whether you're ready for it or not. We need to have a mindset of attack every single day. Think this, your business has an immune system. If your immune system is strong, when any external attack happens, you have the strength to fight, you have the reserve to fight, you have the tenacity to fight because the business is healthy.

Can you borrow confidence if you don't have any? Yes! I offered anyone to borrow mine during the pandemic, confidence, belief, faith and optimism. I kept saying, "You can pay me back when this is all over."

For us to be salespeople we need to have conviction, belief, and confidence in what we are selling. My favorite line from the talk was, "success is not something you own, it's something you rent." This is such a great phrase, I want to say it again, "success is not something you own, it's something you rent." And that's why confidence is so important to master.

Another definition of confidence is, it is internal, knowing that you can create or manifest what you see in your mind – don't look at things and go "wow I could never do that. That's for them but not for me, like I'm not smart enough, I'm not good-looking enough, I'm not tall enough, I'm not whatever." There are more millionaires made during recessive periods than almost any other period. That's confidence, to act when people say nobody's spending any money. And by the way, Coach told us, "During the last recession was when I was signing bigger contracts."

If you want to connect, reach out at *coachburt.com*

20

MAY 2020

APRIL WAS A POWER-PACKED MONTH of learning. I was waking up grateful, every day. I started to join the dots, why had all these amazing people agreed to help me? The stories they told, were giving me more courage at a time when most of the people around me were starting to lose theirs. The words running through my head were, "be more interested in others," and "you have to give more value out than you ask for in return." I realized my prey drive was waning and needed sharpening, and despite a tough couple of months, I was still full of faith rather than fear. I kept telling the teams that we had to make small adjustments daily to stay on track and that this was the only way we would get out of this mess in one piece. The numbers 1116 were playing in my head; this is something I use often, now to help people make better decisions.

As the month passed, we were still in lockdown. I was going a little stir-crazy. Deaths on the rise, the government running around like headless chickens. We were all sitting at home, waiting. In the UK,

Captain Tom raised millions for charity on his hundredth birthday. Hope and belief were in slim rations.

By the middle of the month, we got the okay to return to the office. Very few members of the team actually wanted to come back, they were comfortable in their pajamas and the mood of fear had spooked everyone. After working with Dr. Mark Goulston, I penned the following which I use to keep me focused:

Be generous of spirit and deed, ask for nothing in return and eventually the right people will beat a path to your door. Don't get discouraged by the wrong people who might get there first.
– Simon Leslie

My Starbucks mug pictures on Instagram continue, fourteen talks are organized for May; it's going to be another cracking month. Riots in HK over China, and over in the US there was looting and also protesting at the brutal killing of George Floyd. Cities under siege and set alight. Towards the end of the month, countries started to talk about loosening the lockdowns. This could be over soon. How wrong were we?

Four of my elite sales team decided to walk from London to Brighton (one hundred kilometers) to bond.

We picked up two in the middle of the night, and another two made it to the seaside, a truly momentous achievement. That team would ensure we kept the lights on during the pandemic and I am grateful for their grit, commitment, and determination. Thank you Andrew Meader, David Serra, Tim Fredd and Nicolo Carofiglio.

21

AN OLYMPIAN CHAPTER

MAY 1, 2020

A conversation with
CARLA DEVLIN

MY COLLEAGUE, STEVE ROWBOTHAM, says you have to get Carla to speak, she's not a public speaker, but her story is unbelievable. Let's do it, I say, the more inspiration the better. They were both British Olympic rowers. Steve ran this interview and I watched in awe, with a box of tissues close by.

Steve, introduces an Olympian and reality TV star, and not just any reality star, one that put herself through the grueling SAS training.

This was a wonderful conversation. I don't think we had another speaker who portrayed so much honesty, authenticity, and relatable human connection as Carla did. Forget all the professional speakers, she confessed this was her first presentation to a group of people, other than a gathering of five-year-olds.

"It's not about how much money is in your bank account that means you are wealthy, it's about making the most of our lives, it's about the personal connections which really matter...

I looked deep into my soul to find a subject to talk about, and could only come up with the fact that I was becoming just like my mother and liked to talk and connect with people. As part of this soul-searching, my connecting with people revealed one of my neighbors was a mentor – you never know the skills and talents people who are closest to you have unless you connect and ask!

The advice I got from this neighbor was to remember a time when you were at your best, when you were achieving things, and the moments you are most proud of. I was asked to recognize the inner chatter – the words I was saying to myself, and the traits I applied during those moments. The neighbor called this the 'inner genius'. When I recognized and understood my inner genius, I could strip life back to what is most important, the stuff which really matters, and apply it during times of chaos. This is what we need to do right now.

I was a kid who didn't fit in, stuck out like a sore thumb, I was geeky and not comfortable in my own skin. Whilst at boarding school in Scotland, I enjoyed the early starts, the dips in the freezing lochs, and regular highland runs. I began to change. The school motto said no matter how hard you pushed yourself, there was always more you could give and learn about yourself, and I started to apply this to my life. My mother also told me, 'As long as you have given your best, it doesn't matter what the outcome is', and mothers are always right! I carried this mindset throughout my life as a mother, a wife, and a sportswoman. It's okay to fail and to make mistakes. Be grateful for the small things and have a growth mindset – learning is not fixed, and know that failure is never permanent.

When I was at university I started to fit in, surrounded by other people just like me – in height, strength, and in attitude. This was my time to work out who was the best version of myself. I began rowing as a sport. I didn't believe I had extraordinary talent, what I did have was a love for rowing, determination, perseverance, and a vision of what I wanted – to race at the Olympics.

With this focus, I moved to London and trained full-time, twice a day, seven days a week, whilst holding down a part-time job. I sacrificed my personal and social life to focus on what I had set her mind on - giving myself one year to be selected. I never wanted to be one of those people who had any regrets.

In 2005, as part of the women's British rowing team, I competed at the World Championship, and was focused on being selected for the 2008 Olympic team. I thought, *If I'm going for it, then I really go for it.* You cannot control the weather, the lane you are in, the competition, or your teammates. What you can control is what is in your control – your sleeping, your eating and drinking, and your mindset. Those controllable factors give you marginal gains, the one percent which separates winning from losing.

As part of my focus in 2007 I won a bronze medal in the World Championship and qualified for my dream, to row at the Olympics. But things never go to plan. In December 2007, I was diagnosed with overtraining syndrome and told to go home and rest. Then two days before Christmas, my dad sadly passed away. My gratitude for being at home at the time was humbling. I just knew deep in my gut that the right thing to do was to start training again – I could either wither away and be sad, which I was, or I could do what my father would have wanted and get back in the boat. After six months of hard training, I secured my seat in the Olympic team.

The Olympic experience in Beijing wasn't about the result, it was the journey. It was about the comradeship and the experiences. For me, it was about being in that moment, being present and being the best version of myself, and helping my teammates be the same. I knew that, at any time, someone could have been better and faster than I was, and that was okay, as long as I had put in the hard work and done my best.

On race day, despite knowing they could produce a fast time, we didn't, and I said 'That's okay' – often in that moment, on the day you just need a bit of luck, and all things to fall into place. Many of my teammates still carry the baggage of failure from that day, yet I rest easy with it and am proud of what we achieved.

I may not have won a medal at the Olympics, but shortly after, Jonny, my long-term boyfriend, asked me to marry him. Shortly after the engagement, chaos struck again, and my mother was diagnosed with cancer and given only a short time to live. The wedding had been planned seven months in the future, but with this tragic news we decided to bring the date forward and gave ourselves a week to organize the event. The dress, venue, and food were organized in seven days, and my mother walked me down the aisle. It was magical!

Two weeks later, bedbound, my mother passed away. After her death, my little sister, Christiana, moved in with us. Previously she was looked after by her mother, as Christiana had Down syndrome. I found it strange that after my mother's death, people were asking 'Where is Christiana going to go?' I was shocked, 'Where do you think she is going to go? She is part of our family and going to go with me' – it was just the right thing to do.

Fast forward and my 'motley crew' and my 'company of

chaos' were demanding much of my time. So I started a full-time job as a business development manager. Though shortly after joining, I was diagnosed with breast cancer. This obviously knocked me off my feet and I was shaken to the core.

I had to approach my illness and treatment with an Olympian mindset. I took every opportunity I could find, and left no stone unturned, looking for every morsel of advantage and gain. I set myself marginal gains, walking the fifteen flights of stairs to the therapy unit every session, and timed myself each week, looking to improve my time. The treatment was like having an ice cream headache for three hours. People advised me to take drugs to dull the pain. I had to be in control of my outcome, I drove myself there and back home for every treatment. I needed to be a mother when I got back and had little ones to look after. I need this to be over as quickly as possible. I need to regain my life, my fitness, my health, my boundless energy. I need to be the mum I was made to be, the aggressor, the strong and caring wife.

I couldn't control the therapy, so I quickly decided to deal with what I could control. Changing the language I used when facing cancer; it wasn't about bashing, crushing and fighting, those words were not authentic to me. My language was about rocking up every day, one foot in front of the other, and being the best version of myself.

As well as the kids, I needed something else positive to

work towards. Cancer is all-consuming and the focus of all conversations. I saw a Channel 4 program – SAS: Who Dares Wins, a reality quasi-military training program. They were asking for people from the general public to apply to be part of an SAS training program. I applied thinking, Even if my application isn't accepted, at least the training I would have to do to be prepared would speed up my recovery. That would be positive and a win-win. My story and drive appealed to the producers so much I was accepted. I got to the last four.

The journey during the show reinforced all my beliefs and experiences from being an Olympian. With hindsight, it's about the inner genius, going with your gut, and having confidence and the marginal gains which helped her get through to the final four in the program. I fondly remembered crying during training and during the backward jump off a three-meter diving board. I focused on each moment, and the fact that there were others with me who I didn't want to let them down so I just got on with it – once I did that, I knew I could do anything.

Under pressure is where you see the best and most raw version of yourself.

It's your ability to be you under pressure which matters when others around you are struggling. It's about making decisions, communicating, trusting your instincts. Being nervous is okay. Believe in yourself if you don't know who else is going to.

> There have been many moments of chaos in my life. We all will face tragedy in our lives and it's the way we respond to it rather than react to it which changes the outcome."
>
> **- CARLA DEVLIN**

Carla's story should resonate with us all, and we were honored to have her share her personal experience with us. We are not alone; talk to people and keep it simple. Go with your gut, control what you can, and keep moving forward one step at a time.

I listened to every one of her words, and as the pandemic got worse, I heard them reverberate through my head. What Carla has achieved is sensational, we just had to beat this battle with the virus.

SAS: Who Dares Wins was a grueling experience and Carla once again showed her true grit and determination all the way through the series. The show is brutal and savage and she was a wonderful competitor.

Carla truly is a superwoman. We were all touched by her story. You can be too, follow her *@carladevlin15* on Instagram.

22

SAY IT AS YOU SEE IT

MAY 4, 2020

A conversation with
MICHAEL SERWA

MICHAEL IS THE SELF-PROCLAIMED most expensive coach in the UK. I can't remember exactly how we met, I liked him but never quite ended up working together. I later hired him to work with a few of my senior people. Then one day I went to see Simon Sinek and we bumped into each other and rekindled our friendship. Michael is confident and brash, not everyone's cup of tea. I'll never forget the line he told me: "In everything I do I aim for perfection and I occasionally settle for excellence." He was excellent on this day.

"You can have it all! I believe, beyond any doubt, that I can be anyone, have anything, and be with anyone I want...

I also believe that everything I've got, you can have too. And more. If you're willing to do the work, that is. Growing up relatively poor in Poland, I left school at seventeen, which in Poland was unheard of, as you needed a degree to get a job in McDonald's. My parents and friends were extremely concerned, and my future looked very uncertain. So, I decided to move to London, the place of opportunity. When I arrived, I could barely speak English, I didn't have any money, and was very reliant on people I knew there. What I did have though was an attitude and focus of I'm here and I am going to dominate, and build the life I want to have, and my parents couldn't give me. When it comes to positive mental attitude, there are two categories that influence it: **External Factors** and **Internal Factors**.

When things are not going our way, we look at external factors to blame. When we do this we lose control, we lose power, and we put ourselves in a victim position. We let those external factors change the way we feel and therefore are not in a situation to change them.

When we accept that we are in control of our attitude

and the internal factors, then we are in a far better position to make good decisions, right decisions, and the right choices, as it's coming from a positive place. With a positive mental attitude, we take responsibility for the good or bad things that happen to us and know that we have the power to control them or the way we think about them. Successful people are not happy because of external factors, they are happy because of internal factors and the decision they have made to be happy.

Being responsible for our attitude needs to be constantly worked on and maintained. Some days, especially in the mornings, I wake up without a positive mental attitude for no particular reason. I just cannot put my finger on it. So I stop looking for the reasons and just accept that sometimes, no matter who you are, we just don't feel happy. In those moments, cultivate qualities regardless of how you feel. You should ask yourself; *how do I feel about this? What can I do about it?* You have the power to change your perception of how you feel in that moment. By taking responsibility for this, you can discipline yourself to stay positive, by looking for reasons to feel good about yourself and your life.

To have a positive mental attitude, we need to review all parts of our lives and not just work. If work isn't aligned with what you want, you spend forty hours a week waiting for Friday and dreading Monday. If you have a toxic relationship which you don't want, you hate Fridays and long for Mondays. Also, consider career, finances, family, friends, interests, passion, and health. Ask yourself, on a scale of one to ten, how happy are you in those areas? One means extremely dissatisfied with the status, ten being extremely satisfied. Take responsibility to change your score. This is a very interesting exercise and one I do regularly to ensure nothing will slow me down.

Every minute spent with a negative person is a minute not spent with a positive person. Why spend time with people who make us feel bad about ourselves? Spend time with people who make you feel good about yourself.

What's really important is to be happy with what you have right now, while pushing yourself towards the pursuit of what you want.

These are my life mantras:
- It is what it is.
- Assume nothing, confirm everything.
- Create your expectations and raise your standards.
- Discipline yourself to stay positive as much as you can.
- 80% of life is showing up."

- MICHAEL SERWA

To reach Michael, visit *michaelserwa.com*

23

CULTURE IS KING

MAY 6, 2020

A conversation with
GARRY RIDGE

GARRY RUNS A BIG public company and is a hugely successful leader. I was delighted to pick his brain during this period. He gave me a big, broad shoulder to lean on. Everyone talks about culture, and Garry talks the talk and walks the walk. As CEO of WD-40 since 1997, Garry Ridge has helped re-ignite excitement and create cultures that foster break-through innovation in companies and workplaces in over sixty-two countries. In his no-nonsense Australian style, he has attributed his success to having a culture of purpose-driven people that are learners and have a set of values that keep them on track with focus and clarity.

Garry beautifully opened his time with us.

"We have to forgive others for being human. There are lots of viruses in organizations where people are just not prepared to say things to others; we have a duty of care to make each other better...

I've never made a mistake in my life. I've had millions of learning moments. Every mistake is a teachable moment. We are going to stumble over things and experience things we have never experienced before – and we have to learn from them. I want to talk about servant leadership, as leaders of teams or of ourselves. The leader's job is to enable those that they lead to achieve their goals. Tiger Woods' coach never put on the green jacket at the Masters or ran onto the course. And more importantly, he never was at the podium picking up the prize. He was at the podium, supporting Woods' win.

You need to be tough-minded and tender-hearted. If your child came home from school with a bad report card, would you fire them from the family? No, you would coach them and help them in any way you could. Leaders need to have a heart of gold, but they also have a backbone of steel. We need to care about the wellbeing of our people.

Some time back, I was in a leadership meeting. One of our

leaders was not creating positive, lasting memories in that meeting. In fact, they were exuding a toxic attitude. At the end of the meeting, I said to this person - let's call him Joe - 'Hey, Joe, can we go for a walk? We walked out to the parking lot, and I looked in a trash can and I looked behind the car and I looked behind a tree, and Joe asked me 'what the hell are you doing?' 'I'm looking for you,' I answered, 'The Joe I know and love was not in that room.

Joe explained to me that he had a bad morning and that he was really sorry. 'I had a bad morning. I hit my foot on the bed, I spilled coffee on my crotch, I got flipped off in the car, I had no right to bring that into the meeting.'

So I did a little coaching. I said, 'I'm having this conversation with you because you signed up to the value of creating positive, lasting memories and you have not been accountable for this'. Joe, after that conversation, went back and visited with those who were in that meeting, and he asked for their forgiveness. A classic learning moment for all of us.

Imagine a place where you go to work and make a contribution to something bigger than yourself, you learn something new, you're protected and set free by a set of clear values; that's my belief about a good business. As leaders, we need to be responsible for and build this in our businesses. Culture equals our values multiplied by our behavior and the consistency in applying these.

How did you build the culture at WD-40?

I didn't impose the values, we developed them and agreed on them as a team. Together we went through a process of defining: what did we want to be proud of? We wanted to come up with five or six ranked values that described behaviors that we thought would build an enduring company over time. Then we shared with the teams. We asked, how do these feel to you? Do you understand them? We had a couple of iterations. It took us about nine months. We had 'lunch and learns' where we said, if one value was doing the right thing, what would that look like? How would we describe it? Then for each of our values we created a paragraph that describes what it means and how it could be interpreted, particularly in different countries and cultures. We embedded them into the business in everything we did so that everybody started to use them and live with them daily. One of the most important things we ask every ninety days is what we do every day, whether it aligns with our values, and how we have lived those values during that period.

We call ourselves a tribe, a tribe is a group of people that come together to help protect and feed each other. One of the biggest desires we have as human beings is to belong. Have you left a party, an organization, or even a relationship because you didn't feel like you belonged because you felt like you were an outsider?

One of my favorite movies is The Godfather. I've been

really interested in understanding the background of the Mafia tribe and how it works. Guess what it's all about: values. Even the Mafia has values. We wouldn't agree with the values they had, yet the one thing I do know is they are being enforced. Values are an attribute of being a tribe. I believe that we feel more comfortable around people who share values like ours.

I watched a documentary about drug addicts in the Bronx, New York. I would feel very uncomfortable in that environment, but the people that were there felt very comfortable in that space because those were the values they shared. In my business, we have complete clarity around what we expect from each other, and we have zero tolerance around individuals not embodying our values. We hold each other accountable. It helps us have conversations that are meaningful. Not a conflict.

What are your leadership secrets?

I take full responsibility as a tribal leader. My role is to be a learner, a teacher, and to have a future focus. If you analyze indigenous tribes globally, this is what keeps people together over many years.

As a leader, I remain and am comfortable with being 'consciously incompetent'. I learned the three most important words in my life, many years ago - 'I don't know'. I believe the guy at the top should not be the smartest guy.

I am also very disciplined. I set a daily agenda; I make sure

I am focused on what I need to get done, because distraction is easy. I am also disciplined enough to be able to take a break, talk to the dog for a while, and take a walk out in the garden to free my mind.

No lying. No faking. No hiding. Treat people with respect and dignity, do what you promised to do. Set boundaries, set discipline, and allow freedom. Take care of the people you are in charge of, don't be 'in charge' of your people.

Leaders love the gift of feedback. When your mother says to you, 'Can I give you a bit of advice?' You know, whether you want that advice or not, you're going to get it, and we need to say, 'Thank you for the feedback, Mom', because she cares about you and that's all feedback is. It's about caring. We must stop the brain going into auto mode and move from 'how am I going to defend myself?', 'I'm not going to believe what you're telling me', and forming a rebuttal, to just listening and saying thank you."

- GARRY RIDGE

I practice gratitude daily. I write notes and tell people how grateful I am. I let people know I am thinking of them. Garry asked us a powerful question: "Who would you call if you knew you were going to die today?" Why wait – call them today. We have so much to be grateful for. Garry tells us of a podcast he was listening to; "a woman lost her husband to a cardiac arrest using a treadmill." The host said, "things could be worse. You have a lot to be grateful for," and she blew up and said, "What do you mean I have a lot to be grateful for?" He said, "Your husband died of a cardiac arrest on a treadmill, that could have happened in your car, with your three children, and all of them may have died." Still having your children, that is something to be grateful for.

Help your people to get an A. Let me tell you a story of what I mean. I had a situation many years ago when we let someone go in a particular department. I called up the leader and asked, "Could you share with me and give me the plan on what you did to help them be successful?" They didn't have a plan. I said to the leader, "We let that person down, because we were too lazy to keep our commitment to make this work."

Finding the right people to join our tribe is very important. We go through a lot of processes when we bring people into the company. That doesn't mean someone won't slip through the net occasionally. Everything we do is to promote our tribe and values. If you go on our careers website, the first thing that pops up is our tribe. This is what we stand for, here are our values. We say to people, 'If you don't align with these, don't bother to call us'.

On a regular basis, I ask myself, 'What fifteen things can we do to change our business?' It helps with being mindful and creatively, intentionally curious.

A great leader has no ego. Instead of ego they have empathy. Have empathy for others, it means that we are committed to and we care about the success in the world. Garry's message in leadership and culture is not theoretical, it's practical, and the proof of its importance is in the results. Culture needs accountability and consistency. Garry tells us, don't just give it lip service, make it the most important thing and then people align with it and believe in what we believe.

It was a great reminder of how far we have to go to have the culture I want at Ink. A culture where people know what to do, even when they don't have instruction or direction.

Connect with Garry at *thelearningmoment.net*

24

TIME TO CHECK WHERE WE ARE

MAY 10, 2020

A conversation with
CHRIS HUGHES

CHRIS HAD BEEN my coach for over a decade, and we remain great pals. He checked in with me every month during this period. He lives in the most beautiful part of the British Isles and every time I really need some thinking time, I go and see him, hike, and catch up. I was honored to have him to come and talk to the group.

He started the talk by asking the team what they learned from the previous speakers, and the feedback was super powerful. The team was engaged.

"How long does it take for the average person to get a black belt? The answer is never. An average person cannot do it!...

DON'T BE AVERAGE.

My purpose is maximizing the potential of others while working. Family: nourish their soul, bring out the best version of themselves.

People don't achieve because the outcome isn't in alignment with the purpose. If it is, it is a natural flow. Outcome + purpose = expected outcome. If you are not getting the outcome you want, then you need to re-calibrate. You need to be willing to make corrections along the way and stick to them. If we died now, could we say the last week was a good week? If not, then make adjustments.

To keep focused on the outcomes, ask yourself: 'What do I want to do today?' And this has to be aligned with your focus. Even on days when you don't feel like doing it, you will know you need to do it, and this will control your state. Just go forward because movement is crucial. The danger is we get stuck in a rut, and what is the difference between a rut and a grave? The only difference is how deep it is! Your behavior is your true intention.

Alignment is the key. For me, it's about serving others, being grateful, enjoying achieving, and showing up fully in everything I am engaged with. We have to be fully present, focused on doing whatever I am doing in the moment, then I end up with outcomes, and this leads me to my next purpose.

DON'T LISTEN TO CEDRIC!

Even when we are tapping into that inner place of alignment, the negative part of the brain starts to shout. It will shout about problems when there are none – Cedric is the name I give that part of the brain, and it is a great observer in finding potential problems and issues which are not there. In those moments that Cedric shouts loud, all you need to do is talk to him and say, 'Thanks Cedric, but now fuck off!'

FOCUSING ON TRUSTING AND 'SOLUTION THINKING', ASK YOURSELF THESE QUESTIONS:

- What is the issue?
- What can I do about it?
- What can't I do about the issue?

Then let go of the stuff you cannot do, focus on the can-dos and not on the can't-dos.

Think of energy as a currency – work out when you are at your best and maximize your energy to get the best results during that time. Even at times when you feel less resourceful, know from your core, it's going to be okay.

There is unlimited energy at this core due to the depth of creativity and resources. Go into nature, it will fuel your energy, get good sleep, and manage what is coming into the body as it affects what is coming out. Be mindful of what you consume in all aspects of life, not relying on stimulants. Being obsessed about your outcome and purpose gives you the fuel that keeps you going."

- CHRIS HUGHES

Reach out to Chris at *thehughescompany.co.uk*

25

A LESSON OF KINDNESS

MAY 11, 2020

A conversation with
ADRIENNE BANKERT

I SAW ADRIENNE TALK on Dave Meltzer's show and I loved her message. I reached out and thankfully she agreed to come and talk to the team. We couldn't have had a better guest to share the concept of 'kindness as a superpower'.

Adrienne was great in the early morning, she shone on the screen with her amazing grace, style, and smile. An Emmy award-winning journalist and national correspondent for ABC News, she now presents a primetime show on NewsNation.

She started her talk about creating safe spaces for people to be themselves amongst all this chaos and crisis – We should have done this before the pandemic. This safe space is about having kindness for yourself and others. In that space, we are the most authentic.

"Imagine being at a party, and people are asking what you do. When people hear I am a journalist they often give me a wide berth, as they think they need to be careful what they say when around me. No, I am just human. We all have the same challenges, shock, awe and feeling totally disconnected...

In my business, we all need real social interaction. Not just a face on a screen, but real connection with people, where we can look in the eyes of someone who knows and understands us. The lockdown stopped this.

What do journalists know about the elevator pitch?

I once interviewed Brad Pitt. Imagine this, Brad has been interviewed a zillion times. So how do you make yourself different, gain his trust, and get him to open up to you? And with only thirty seconds to do it? The technique I used with him and others is to be kind, thoughtful, considerate, and friendly. It's developmental, it's practice, it's a lifestyle, but it has now become who I am.

During lockdown, I felt as if all my communication was

becoming automated and impersonal. It became just words – I hope you are healthy and safe during the crisis? – I couldn't go out and see friends and interact with them. It felt like I was losing who I was and couldn't come up with a solution. Finally, it dawned on me; I said, 'Why don't I read my own book?' I wrote a chapter in it on, 'the kindness to keep you from going crazy'?" I realized that to solve my isolation problem, I should solve other people's problems first and serve them with kindness.

I decided to connect with faces and send selfie video messages, saying hello, I care, and I love you. My recommendation is to be different from other organizations, who will be emailing, and then emailing more. Record videos, show your clients during this time that you care, invest time building on the relationship, put a smile on their faces, and tell them you remember them. This is wonderful advice whatever the market condition, stand out and be you.

It's not about what you do. It's not about what you've accomplished. It's not who your friends are. It's that I will never meet another you on this planet for the rest of my life.

I am a 'connection expert' and the superpower to release this was kindness. I had a professional relationship with a cameraman at one point, who one day butt-called me. I knew he had health issues and he lived on his own, with his daughters close yet unable to visit him due to lockdown. I thought, how could I approach the call with kindness? Rather than just asking if he was safe and healthy during the pandemic, I wanted to show him I cared. So, I thanked him for the call and said to him, 'I'll adopt you, and if it's okay I'll check in on a regular basis'. I could feel the love and kindness reflected on the call.

At this time, we need to stop treating people - customers, colleagues, and friends - as ways to improve the bottom line. We need to treat them like family and friends – there is no room to be lonely right now, adopt people and be responsible for them. Kindness is not something we just teach our children and ignore as adults. Let's put kindness in the workplace; it's universal and inclusive.

It's not about the power of one, it's about all the people you cannot see in the room. All the people who have helped you get to where you are, the army of support behind you. You must honor those that have helped you and who will help you get to where you want to be – family, friends, we are responsible for their time and investment. When you remember this, you will walk into any room with confidence.

If we are too honest, we're more concerned about just being ourselves, and less concerned about connection. Continue to be honest, but if you put kindness and connection ahead of that honesty, you'll make better decisions of what to share and what not to share in that moment.

What does 'shake it off like Brad Pitt' mean? When I asked him when he plays a depressing role, does it affect him? Brad said he just shakes it off to change his state – so whenever I get gloomy, I remember to shake it off like Brad, telling myself how fortunate I am. I say to myself, How amazing you are, because nobody else is going to do it for you. And then I sing the song from the musical Oklahoma! 'Oh, what a beautiful morning. Oh, what a beautiful day. I've got a beautiful feeling, everything's going my way.' It's easier to remember a song mantra so find your favorite tune and just sing the lyrics.

I remember when, early in my career, one day a sound engineer snapped at me and was rude; I wanted to respond in the same way, yet stopped myself. The next day I found out that the engineer's mother had died, and he came to work anyway. When someone is rude to you, you never really know why. Sometimes, bad things happen. Growing up with six siblings, I was used to just snapping back, but now, with a kindness understanding, I have been able to stop that retaliation reaction.

Kindness is about understanding. My mentor, Bill Kraus, told me I must learn every role involved in my craft. In front of and behind the camera. Through understanding the pressure of each role and the role from their point of view, you can lead with kindness. It's not just about being kind to the star, as Will Smith said. Be kind to everyone, whether they look like they can help you or not. No longer is it about I'll scratch your back, you scratch mine – that isn't kindness. True kindness is doing things for people who can never pay you back.

To make kindness your lifestyle, as you will be so shocked by the kinds of people you get to meet, the different doors of opportunity which open, and the help you get down the road. The world is in a different place, demanding that we are kind under pressure and we have an opportunity to do this. Organizations are changing to want more respect for one another, approaching performance holistically by demanding more compassion.

Dreams are really important. As is having a vision of what you want and being explicit about it. There is power in having a vision board. When my friends helped her unpack boxes in my new apartment, they stumbled on a scrap of paper saying I wanted to write a book. I now see this wasn't explicit enough – after all, writing a book is not the same as being a published author. Make your vision board not a framework, but a picture. It's not just about objects; include relationships, who you want to be, and the people you want to be with. Be intentional and full of kindness.

Kindness has motivated me to do anything to achieve my dreams. There was a particular negotiation with a studio, where I pushed too hard during a negotiation and they didn't take my contract. Because I needed an income, I became a hostess in a local restaurant to pay the bills. It so happened the producer who was part of the negotiation came in one lunchtime. I didn't know how to approach the woman, so approached her with kindness and my authenticity kicked in. When the woman asked why I was working in the restaurant I answered, 'I host on TV and I am hostess here; let me show you to your table.' I was offered a contract two weeks later.

Sell pencils on a street corner, flip burgers, you have to do whatever it takes. Kindness isn't always neat and tidy. It's not about where you are, it's about why you're there. It's the days which matter - the connections you make, knowing people matter, the days when you're feeling down and someone opens a door for you, buys you coffee or shows they care with kindness - they matter. Old people talk of worlds getting smaller. That's not true; if you neglect your friends and don't stay in touch with them, then the world gets smaller, times go faster, and before we know it five years have passed and we haven't been in touch. We have to be intentional with our relationships.

What advice would you give your younger self?

A lesson for us all – stop hiding who you are and your gifts. Don't worry about making mistakes – if you do, you'll make them anyway. Mistakes are going to happen; if you understand this, you will not freak out when they do.

Kindness is a word used often and not often delivered. Adrienne is a perfect example to us all of the power of kindness. Her hidden superpower is indeed as a connection expert. To engage 150 complete strangers via Zoom and make us feel like we were sitting in her kitchen, having a chat with a best friend reflects kindness in practice. Help customers (we should call them friends, perhaps) with kindness and friendship, don't worry about the bottom line."

- ADRIENNE BANKERT

Many of the messages Adrienne shared with us are in her book, *Your Hidden Superpower:* The Kindness that Makes You Unbeatable at Work and Connects You with Anyone, which highlights the lessons she has learned first-hand about compassion, facing competition, and dealing with negativity at work and in life. Her refreshing perspective on kindness is practical and revelatory, covering identity and establishing authentic connections. She tells us kindness keeps you creative and innovative. It keeps you from going crazy, and focuses you on serving people and working out how you can solve their problems. The more people you help, the more you will achieve whatever it is you want.

We all love this metaphor she shared: "a picture frame without a picture in it is just a frame."

She told us she wrote the book to explore the idea of winning without creating rivals. She realized that if we were all kind to each other then we would never have to compete again. We can all have a different type of kindness, a thumbprint unique to us – we all remember the flight attendant, doctor or teacher who was kind. It's our authentic value, because you are delivering something that no one else delivers. Therefore, the world needs you because you deliver something that no one else delivers – and that something is you! Think about that as you go forward – what version of you do you want to show up?

Who would I be if I didn't have problems? This is the type of question you should be asking yourself.

You can follow Adrienne *@ABonTV* on Instagram

26

HOW SHOULD YOU LOOK AND BEHAVE?

MAY 12, 2020

A conversation with
SANDY GRIGSBY

MY MATE, SANDY GRIGSBY, came and talked about getting that look right, and boy, I need her to do my long-overdue transformation.

Welcome to the queen of authenticity; Sandy oozes confidence and reflects her energy in every aspect of her physical and mental beiwng. She shared with us how, by having a full body makeover, we can come closer to who we really are, we can build deeper connections, show up as the best version of ourselves, and achieve more. She told us of her personal story of discovering who she is. Sandy describes herself as a personal brand engineer; she works with people, identifying what they stand for and what their true identity is.

"It's moving from the influences based on life experiences, who we have met – people, parents, friends, partners, spouses – but that doesn't mean that we've made the right choices. We have to look deeper into ourselves and create a new dynamic for what we think we are...

I practice what I preach – I would never tell you to do something that I haven't done. I used to have super low confidence as a little girl, life started to beat me down. I was sexually assaulted at a very young age. I had bad relationships with men. I had bad relationships with women. I was sexually harassed at work, I had to quit multiple jobs to get away from the sexual harassment. I was very shy for a while, I didn't have the confidence to speak up for myself, I was in a domestic violence situation with my partner. I had to actively change my situation, change my habits, and deep-dive into what it was that was keeping me in that state of unhappiness. With insight, I realized this just wasn't me! And I questioned myself on how I could shift from being that person to the one I wanted to be.

I read a lot of books, went to a lot of workshops, and had therapy. I worked on myself to really uncover what my issues were and what I needed to do to pull out my best self.

A way of doing this is to go back in time, to when you were a little kid, four or five years old. Think of those first few memories. What were you like? What kind of kid were you? Were you super tender and sweet to other kids, or were you that naughty kid, that kid that likes to stir up some trouble? Now, write down the kind of kid that you were, and then ask yourself, are you the same person now that you were as a little kid? Think of who you were and who you are, and think of how it's shifted. What was lost over time? Contemplate how much you can change.

Another exercise to do is think of your favorite animal. If you can't decide, choose whatever animal comes to mind. Think of three adjectives to describe that animal, but not things like brown, tall, and hairy. My favorite animal is a giraffe. Graceful, serene, and protective. Once you have those words, think: do those words describe me? And how often do we show up as those words?

I would also think about the times when I was happiest; I think about the times when people told me that they really loved me, and it was when I was a gregarious, confident, playful person.

Now we have completed those exercises, remember the answers and let's figure out who you are now and who you want to be. All these exercises will help you achieve that.

Who are you and how do you show up in the world? Who do you want to be, and how do you want to show up? How do we create a beautiful personal brand that we can commit to and be? It's the practices that create the showing up you. If you don't love something about yourself, it's time to sit with yourself and figure out what that is. Decide who you want to be, and then put into place little bitty habits to get you there.

And now the fun starts.
To begin the realization process, create a mood board. The easiest way of doing this, is to go to Pinterest, do searches, and pin things that you love, such as locations for a vacation. Look for the rooms, the buildings, office spaces, environments, and gardens.

It doesn't matter what it is, but find things that you love, because what you're doing is subconsciously creating who you are. When I did this, I realized the board reflected a completely different brand from the way I was showing up. From the way that I lived, the way that my home looked, and what I was wearing, it was all different. The mood board had colors and all I wore was black and dark colors. It just wasn't me. I changed, I started wearing soft pinks and peachy colors and blues and grays and a lot of white, and just really light, soft colors. People told me, 'You used to wear a lot of black and it just didn't feel like it was you'. The same was true for my mom.

She was moving from San Jose, California, to Las Vegas. She had bought a brand-new condo, and, in her mind, she wanted really dark furniture, dark lamps, everything was big and dark. That just wasn't her. That's not my mom. I sat with her and created a mood board. It was totally the opposite of that dark she claimed to like. She changed her designs and now she is happier in her space.

One thing to remember is that we tend to go through ten-year cycles. If you consider who you were ten years ago, you are very different now. So, you need to repeat the mood board exercise.

What's deeply seated inside of us will allow our best selves to shine. We have no excuse to not be the best versions of ourselves because we are what we create.

What happens if there are moments when we are not the best versions of ourselves?

Grab a journal, grab a notebook, grab a piece of paper, grab your phone, and write down what you're most grateful for. Because when you start doing this daily exercise of gratitude, it allows you to see the best version of you. Gratitude helps you to start living in the good moments, as opposed to nestling in moodiness and the bad moments. You can reprogram and reset your brains. Writing in a journal, you reset yourself, you can fire up your brain to create the best version of you. You have the choice to be in a bad mood and to be depressed. You have a choice to feel certain ways, and you have the choice to switch it.

Another thing you could do each and every night, right before bed, is write in another journal three things in that day you accomplished and were proud of. It could be anything, it doesn't have to be a big thing. On days when you're feeling particularly low and you're lacking confidence, go back to that journal and start reading through it. We forget about all of the amazing things that we do on a day-to-day basis, we forget all of those little, tiny things that happen throughout the day that are wonderful and empower us and make us who we are. That will organically boost your confidence.

Another thing to do is remember when you were really good at something. The magic that made you really amazing and successful. A time when you were talking about something you were excited and passionate about, that is when your radiance was coming through. Close your eyes and remember it. This is what you need to call upon when you need to pull up absolute confidence.

Your brand is not just about what you wear and your colors. A big area to remember is your posture. Be straight, elongated. Place your feet firmly planted on the ground, hip-width apart, then I want you to elongate your spine. Stretch your spine up to the sky, high and tall. Next, elongate your neck; you're going to stretch out the neck as though reaching for the stars. Imagine your vertebrae, your spine, and your neck going straight to the heavens, and then I want you to relax your shoulders, keep everything elongated and shoulders down. Then, I want you to stick your head out like a turtle – it looks ridiculous, but I can tell you movie stars, actors on TV, anchors on TV shows, they all do this by default.

Look at those Instagram models that look really fabulous. This is their secret weapon. Stick your face out like a turtle chiseling too high and then bring it down a bit. What this does is it allows your face to come forward to the camera, which shows presence. It shows that you're there, connecting with people. It allows you to look confident, alert, and it brings out the most amazing version of you.

You can also do a superhero pose. To perform the superhero pose, spread your legs to take a wider stance, then put your hands on your hips. Their spines are elongated, their chins forward, and they are stretching to the sky. Hold that for about thirty seconds. Feel the confidence!

What about advice on generic styles?

What color works best for your skin tone? There may be colors from your mood board which just don't look good on your skin, so the way that you correct for that is you just don't wear those colors near your face. You can wear it as some sort of accessory, belt, bag, or have it in the background, it doesn't need to be on your body. You can still incorporate your branding colors without actually having them close to your face. No need to limit yourself on the colors. It's about having fun with it and owning it with confidence.

What about the men? It almost doesn't matter what you're wearing, wear it with confidence. Confidence means you owned it. Remember posture – elongated necks, the shoulders relaxed and chest high. If you're muscular, have pecs, and have nice arms, then tighter clothing tends to look better. If you are very slim, and you don't have a lot of shape, then a little bit looser. And if you are heavier-set, try not to wear things that make you look even bigger. No big baggy clothes. If you're wearing things that are really baggy, then you're just lost in fabric, though it's better to wear things that are not tight.

If you have a longer face, you would want a turtleneck, for guys, a crewneck is great if you have a longer face. The reason for that is, the longer your face, the more it draws the eye down. So, if you have a longer neckline, your face appears even longer. Avoid a V-neck, it's going to make everything seem even longer. If you have a round, short face, then you want the longer neckline, so a V-neck would be great (for women, a long plunging neckline is beautiful if you have a shorter face.) If you have a more medium-sized face – not too long, not too short, and a nice square jawline – you can wear pretty much anything.

What's the difference between confidence and

arrogance? Confidence is knowing you're good at something, arrogance is thinking you're good at something. There's a huge difference. So, if you know you're really good at your job, you are the best at your job, you hit those numbers, you are happy at the end of the day when you do it, you love what you're doing, you're passionate, you can't wait to get started. You're fired up. That's confidence. But if you think you're good at it, and you're talking to other people like you're good at it, you're telling everyone what to do. But when you actually sit down to do the work, you're not passionate about it, you're not fired up, and you kind of question yourself. That's arrogance.

How do you stay true to your style and authenticity when others may criticize you? It's all about committing to it. If someone's going to criticize you, but you feel good in it and you feel comfortable and you love it, then so what? There are things that I've worn in my past that I liked, and people thought I was weird. Whatever, I'm still going to wear it because I love it, and later I find out people appreciated and respected me even more for committing to and being consistent with it, rather than just being wishy-washy. If it's something that you're passionate about and you really love it, you are going to serve the world better by showing up and committing to it."

— SANDY GRIGSBY

All these tips were helpful for all of us. I remember I was once told that I strut around like a cockerel – that wasn't arrogance, that was confidence! And Sandy told us about really good stances to help to show up with confidence.

As a result of her journey of discovery, she shared with us some exercises to find who we really are and who we want to be. If you don't like something about yourself, you have an opportunity in this beautiful life to change everything.

You can follow Sandy at *sandyinfocus.com*

27

FOOD FOR THOUGHT

MAY 13, 2020

A conversation with
JJ VIRGIN

AS I WAS POSTING all the great speakers, more and more people would ring up and suggest other great speakers. Eric Edmeades called me up and said, "You have to have JJ come and talk to your team, she is a firecracker and has a great story."

He was spot on. It was early in Tampa and JJ was bubbling with enthusiasm.

JJ Virgin is a New York Times best-selling author, adviser to the stars on nutrition, a mother, and consultant to the world's leading health organizations.

WARNING – I am certainly not a health expert, and to avoid any misunderstanding of the messages JJ gave, I have selected to share below the top-level themes explored. Please reach out to JJ or a qualified nutritionist for more information.

"We have to think of our bodies as complex science labs and not just tanks to deposit fuel in order to drive our engines. Weeks before my first book was published, my sixteen-year-old son was involved in a car accident, which resulted in a coma and multiple brain bleeds...

I was told that, despite hanging on to life for the time-being, he was going to die sometime in the next twenty-four hours. His injuries were so bad that the surgery he required was very specialized and he needed to be airlifted to another hospital. The doctors told me that he would never survive the airlift, and even if he did and had the surgery, he would be so brain damaged that it wouldn't be worth it.

In that situation, I had to decide 'how to show up' and proceeded to overrule the doctor. My son was airlifted, where he survived the airlift and he survived that first surgery. I had to be determined that I was going to help my son be 110% – and that's what I told him. I'm like, 'Grant, I just need you to fight, because I will pull in every single resource to get you to be 110%'. It was tough to show up in that situation. I remember the first twenty-four hours; complete disbelief, freak-out anger, crying, scared out of my mind. There I am, standing and looking at my son, who is in a coma in the middle of a pediatric ICU, listening to some bells and whistles going off to monitor everything, surrounded by doctors and nurses and wondering how to pull this one off. You see some people showing up, doing incredible things, and then some people showing up as a victim. I held his hand for days, never letting my faith dip.

The good news is that Grant is now well.

So, what can we do to improve our immune systems?

Before you even think about chemistry, understand the importance of positivity and gratitude. When studying patients with HIV, those who practiced gratitude and were disciplined to find positivity significantly saw a drop in their viral load.

Sleep is another way to boost our immune systems. Sleep makes you more insulin-resistant. Go to sleep in a pitch-black room for your body to make that melatonin. Make sure you're not doing stimulating activities right before bed, like watching some scary movie, especially avoid staring at screens. I put the red glasses on for an hour before bed, minimum thirty minutes before, and that has changed my deep sleep dramatically. If you wake up in the middle of the night, don't look at the clock, because you almost start to teach yourself this is the time I wake up. And, finally, it can also help, three to four hours before bed, to eat a balanced meal so that you don't get hypoglycemia that will then cause the stress hormones to dump blood sugar into your bloodstream and wake you back up.

Sugar is a big player in your immune system. The studies show that if you eat sugar, your immune system actually can decline for hours after eating it. We need to get our blood sugar balanced. Eat some clean protein, like wild salmon, grass-fed beef, pastured chicken, and eat some healthy fats like avocado, nuts, and seeds. You should be eating fiber from non-starchy vegetables and a little bit of slow low carbs, maybe things like squash, sweet potato, or wild rice. When you eat that way, you keep your blood sugar balanced. The protein and fiber slow down stomach emptying so you feel fuller longer.

Intermittent fasting is a good way of detoxifying your body and helps get rid of the cellular trash. It helps with the immune system and triggers your body to make more stem cells. It also helps to improve your blood sugar and your insulin sensitivity. So, what is intermittent fasting? For a start, it gives all the benefits of fasting without the pain of fasting. Begin by stopping eating three to four hours before bed. Then you can stretch that overnight, from twelve hours to fourteen hours, to sixteen hours.

We cannot live our lives as victims, regardless of the situations we are faced with. I was determined that my son would never be a victim, that while he was a victim of a hit and run – because the woman who hit him ran him down in the street, got out of her car, gasped, and drove off – I was determined he would not be a victim, that he would only be a victor, and that we would use this as a stepping stone to get to a better place in life.

I also realized, when faced with this situation, that I needed to be stronger and that I had to put myself and my health first. That self-care was critical and had to be prioritized – after all, there was no room for my being sick. It's the most selfless thing I could do. This was not selfish, but a selfless act.

I decided it was all about up leveling your health and immune system; after all, we cannot control many of the illnesses out there, but what we can control is the strength to fight it. You have to say to yourself 'I'm worth it, I have something important to do in the world' and 'I've got purpose'."

- JJ VIRGIN

After her talk, JJ was so gracious, answering individual questions from around the world. I learned so much from the Q&A. She used to sneak fish oil into the hospital to give to her son, and attributes this to his recovery. She is a huge fan of fish oil. If you don't know or follow JJ, I would wholly recommend you do.

You can reach JJ at *jjvirgin.com*

28

LIFE IS A BIG ADVENTURE

MAY 14, 2020

A conversation with
ALISON LEVINE

IT'S BEFORE 6AM in Northern California and we find Alison sitting in her closet. This woman was a bolt of energy as she came on screen. Like someone you have known your entire life.

As most children, I was always inspired by the stories of adventurers, such as Hillary climbing Everest and Scott and Shackleton traveling to the Poles, pushing themselves to mental and physical extremes. With this conversation, we finally got to meet a real adventurer, and we were all captivated by her, her boundless energy, and her stories of pushing the limits of what is possible.

Alison was full of excitement, ready to share her stories. This woman is amazing, she has ascended the highest peaks on every continent, and also skied to both the North and South Poles. In 2010, she completed the Adventure Grand Slam by reaching the summit of Mount Everest. She was asked to serve as the team captain of the first American Women's Everest Expedition. In her spare time, she teaches at the United States Military Academy at West Point. She shares her stories with businesses to help other people become stronger and more resilient, enabling them to face their fears and tolerate failure.

"As a child, I read books and watched documentaries on explorers. Growing up in the heat of Arizona, I am sure that motivated me to seek out some cold weather. Yet, it was all stacked up for failure...

After some health issues and undergoing three heart surgeries, I found out that I suffer from Raynaud's disease. This causes the arteries that feed her fingers and toes to collapse in cold weather, leaving me at extreme risk of frostbite – not the sort of condition for someone who wants to be a polar explorer. But nothing was going to deter me. I decided that if other people can have adventures, then so can I, and at thirty-two I climbed my first mountain: Mount Kilimanjaro.

My biggest critic at the time was myself; I doubted I could do it, and of course, there were other non-believers. All you can do is try to prove them wrong. Like when people tell me I can't do something, that just kind of fuels the fire in me to want to do it. I want to prove them wrong. You have to understand that those people have no say in your life, you are in total control over the things you do and the way you process defeat and failure – after all, failure is the opportunity to learn and go again.

I call it 'failure tolerance'; the lack of it prevents action and stifles performance. An attitude of 'you have to fail to learn' means you can push yourself and persevere when difficult things happen.

A clear example of failure tolerance was when I led the first American Women's Everest Expedition. On our first climb, we did not make it to the summit of Mount Everest. We turned back less than three hundred feet from the summit due to bad weather. It felt like a punch to the gut. It took me eight years to get up the guts to go back and try it again, because I was so afraid of failing. On my second ascent, I reached the summit.

What other experiences while climbing Everest can be used as opportunities for learning and truths for now and the future, for individuals and business?

There was an experience from the Khumbu Glacier. The icefall is considered one of the most dangerous stages of the South Col route to Everest's summit. It is one that forms the icefall and moves at such speed that large crevasses open with little warning, and the large towers of ice (called seracs) found at the icefall have been known to collapse suddenly. People die traversing the glacier. To have fear in this situation is okay; fear is an essential emotion for survival, it's complacency that kills you. It's okay to feel scared or intimidated, because fear is only dangerous if it paralyzes you. Complacency, on the other hand, will kill you every single time. You've got to be able to keep moving, even when you're scared.

You can be scared and brave at the same time. Just keep moving forward.

As you can imagine, there were times on the mountain when I felt overwhelmed. For coping with this, I had a simple strategy: break big tasks down into smaller parts. So, picture the top of Everest; it's over twenty-nine thousand feet above sea level. The high camp is twenty-six thousand feet above sea level. You still have more than three thousand vertical feet to cover to get to the summit. This area is called the 'death zone', the elevation at which human life can no longer be sustained and your body slowly starts to die. At this elevation, you have to take about five breaths for every step. It takes hours and hours and hours just to go a few hundred feet. You just have to put one foot in front of the other. To stop feeling overwhelmed, rather than focusing on the summit, I focused on a rock that I could see down the trail and I thought, *Okay, I just need to get to that rock.* And so, by breaking the whole big something down into smaller parts, it felt so much more doable. I felt like I was making progress. Progress doesn't always feel like progress, but as long as you keep moving forward, it's still progress.

Another thing when you're climbing Mount Everest; you go up and come back down, you go back up and back down until you acclimate your body to the altitude. The other challenge here is the higher you go, the more your muscles deteriorate and the greater the mental challenge of going up and then coming down. At times, you feel like you're losing ground.

But backing up – it's not the same as backing down. Sometimes, you have to back up.

Celebrate the small wins, as I did during my time in the North Pole. Feeling like you're making progress was very difficult. The North Pole is ninety degrees north of the Arctic Circle. It's floating ice, there's no landmass. I would ski for twelve to fifteen hours, then, exhausted, would pitch the tent, and go to sleep. But then you drift because you're just on ice. Sometimes backwards. You wake up the next morning and you are further away than you were the day before when you started. So, it wiped out all your progress and more.

Most of the deaths that occur on Mount Everest, occur after people have reached the summit, because they use everything they've got in them to get themselves to the top and they do not have enough left energy to get themselves down. You have to remember that the summit is halfway, the halfway point. Keep one foot in front of the other for the full journey.

You don't have to be the fastest and you don't have to be the strongest, you just have to put one foot in front of the other. The first woman to ever climb Mount Everest in 1975, Junko Tabei of Japan, said, 'It's not just about technique and ability when it comes to getting to the top. It is willpower, that is the most important, and nobody can give it to you, you cannot buy it, it has to come from your heart.'

Another of my heroes, a trailblazer who battled racism and sexism, and defied political leaders in her quest to become the first Nepali woman to summit Everest, is Pasang Lhamu Sherpa. She shattered the age-old barriers that prevented female Sherpas from climbing. I am the executive producer of a movie about her achievement called The Glass Ceiling. She had the courage to battle the government of her own country for gender and racial equality. Her initial attempts to reach Everest's summit were thwarted by bad weather and climbing politics, but her determination finally paid off when she reached the top on her fourth try in 1993. But triumph turned to tragedy, as Pasang did not make it back down the mountain alive but perished on the descent.

If you have courage you can change a country and a world.

I've compared the challenges faced by everyone during the lockdown to those experienced on many of my adventures and shared the lessons we could apply to help in times like these. It's all about connections, and unlike previous challenges we have faced – 9/11, recession and depression, and my time in the mountains – we could always connect physically, and currently we cannot do that. So, find time to reach out to each other. Communicate – when you're down at Basecamp, that's when you have to motivate people and that's when you have to bring everybody together. And the most important thing is constant communication. That's what creates trust and loyalty. When I was Arnold Schwarzenegger's deputy finance director for his 2003 governor campaign, I had very little to do directly with him, yet he always let me know I was a member of the team and he cared about me as a person. He would walk past me in the corridor and always take the time to ask, 'How is our mountain climber doing today?'

From my time at West Point, I've shared the military phrase of 'VUCA': volatile, uncertain, complex, and ambiguous. We are all uncertain what tomorrow holds and that's okay; what we need to do is focus on what we can control, now and in the moment – one step at a time.

Let me tell you, the South Pole is white, white, and then even more white. There are no landmarks; there are no hints of how far you have gone, the progress you are making, and how far you have to go. It reminds me of being in quarantines. In the South Pole you know you can't quit, and there is no change of scenery. Whilst we cannot quit the lockdown, we can change the scenery. Go outside, rest your body, read. Have a hot bubble bath, do something to pamper yourself. Get champagne and strawberries, take a nap if you need to in the middle of the day, as long as you are getting your work done. Rest your mind, rest your body, and don't feel guilty about doing it.

It's all about the team. On my Antarctic adventure, the team had to travel six hundred miles, pulling a 150lb sled for the entire journey. After five days, I was falling behind and not keeping up with the team. It was basic laws of physics; at five foot four and 112lbs, I just didn't have the bulk to drag 150lb, compared to a six foot three, 230lb person. I was the slowest and weakest person on the team. I felt I was letting my teammates down, that they would be wondering why I was there, and how they could get rid of me. This emotionally hurt me.

What happened next was the best lesson in leadership for us all. One evening I heard the team leader talking. 'Poor Alison, she's really struggling, she's much smaller than everybody. I feel terrible, You know what? I really think we should help her out. I think we should take some weight out of her sled.'

How he handled it was inspiring. Instead of getting out of the tent the next day and saying, 'Alison, I'm taking weight out of your sled,' potentially exposing my weaknesses to the rest of the team, he announced to the team that he wanted to weigh all sleds to make sure the weight was even. 'You have the heaviest sled in the team,' he announced, and then he shared out the load. His leadership skill meant it allowed me to keep my pride, changed the attitude of the teammates by showing I wasn't a hindrance, and in my mind made me want to repay the team back. I just didn't know how. At the end of a twelve-hour track, when you pitch your tent, you have to build a snow barricade around it to protect you from the elements. This is done with a small snow shovel. Tall people would struggle with this, as bending over to build the barricade was painful for them, so I took the responsibility to build everyone's barricades. It's all about playing to your strengths – I was short and found it easier to do.

The lesson here is that within a team everybody has an area where they can shine, everybody has something that they contribute. If we are so focused on comparing ourselves with others in areas where they are strong, we may never really uncover that area where we can truly shine. Your weakness does not determine your value. Never quit. The team is the most important – after all, it's the name on the front of the shirt, not the back, which counts.

I met a student at West Point. It's tough for them, the academic challenges that come with attending university, and they have military training. When I was talking to a young female cadet there, asking about her experience at West Point, the woman said, 'I was torn between West Point and Juilliard, the music school only the most talented musicians can get into'. She said, 'To be honest with you, I don't know that I would have chosen it again. Because there's just days where I feel like I can't do this, where I want to quit'.

A lot of people want to quit, and I think knowing that helps. That vulnerability goes a long way, knowing you are not alone, not the weakest, or not the only person struggling. All the lessons I have had from adventures helped her, and I hope you put some of these towards your life."

- ALISON LEVINE

Do something every day that makes you feel strong. It doesn't have to be something big. It can be something really minor. I do push-ups. Try it and increase the number daily, weekly or monthly. It strengthens your mind and body.

The messages from Alison were so powerful and she gave her time with such love and kindness.

There are always more mountains to climb, and it's important to remember that once you are at the top of one, you have to come down to climb the next. That's life, it's a never ending journey... till the end. Remember, backing up is not the same as backing down. Sometimes you have to back up.

Alison wrote NY Times bestseller, *On the Edge: Leadership Lessons from Mount Everest and Other Extreme Environments. alisonlevine.com*

29

SO MUCH LOVE IN THE ROOM

MAY 15, 2020

A conversation with
TRACEY LIV

TRACEY WAS ANOTHER brilliant introduction. She was full of energy and her message arrived at just the right time in May. I called this week's talks 'the power women week'. Tracey explained the connection between brain and heart and, as a heart-centered leader, I loved this talk. Tracey has continued to keep me centered since 2020 and I find her work fascinating and encouraging. I also admired how Tracey uprooted her family and moved to the Caribbean during the pandemic to liv it!

"I am an American in London. I'll be talking about how to get out of hustle and into alignment in the work that you do...

For alignment we must connect:

- **VISION** – your goal
- **EMOTION** – your inner compass
- **SPIRIT** – your soul compass
- **THE SELF** – your identity
- **THE MIND** – your operating system
- **EXECUTION** – play to your highest potential
- **CHALLENGE** – your personal power

And specifically focus on one powerful technique of heart and mind cohesion.

You probably have a vision and goal for your life, I call it the North Star, somewhere where you want to go. Let me explain my background so you get a clearer understanding of what I mean. I grew up with a lot of financial scarcity. My family was on welfare for large parts of my childhood. I had free and reduced lunches, and I had a coupon to apply for college, because I couldn't afford the seventy-five-dollar application.

My life looked like a tornado; in fact, I was dreaming of

tornadoes every night! It was a really dark place, and I ended up manifesting an eating disorder at nineteen; I was bulimic or I wouldn't eat anything.

Then I was introduced to a healer in Eastern medicine. She was a Reiki healer, and psychic shaman. I thought it was all Voodoo, but essentially, she gave me my power back. She said, 'Tracy, you can work with me, I could do Reiki on you. I can give you herbs, I can talk about your food allergies. I can do all these things. If you keep your current patterns though, I can't help you'. She looked at me and she said, 'You're going to heal yourself'. I had to figure out my own compass and where I was going.

How did my obsession with hockey help me do this? Alexander Mikhailovich Ovechkin is my all-time favorite. He is a Russian professional ice hockey left winger and captain of the Washington Capitals. Often known as 'Ovi' and 'the Great Eight', Ovechkin is widely considered to be one of the greatest ice hockey players of all time. Watching him play taught me about 'inner game'. When he plays, he is completely transcended to somewhere else. He's not in his head. He's in flow. He's in complete alignment. He is a beautiful representation of where hearts and their minds are in complete cohesion. This is what self-mastery in the game is; you've got to refuel, get past fears, grab the courage, and be really aligned to your purpose.

So how do we create heart and mind cohesion?

Understand the brain, it's governed by brainwave states. Beta – using your cognitive thinking skills. It's an alert, active state of mind, problem solving. High range beta – incoherent, anxiety, worry, anger, unable to see clearly, fear, survival, tigers are attacking. Gamma (mid-range beta) – fastest brain waves, peak awareness and experience, high-level cognition and memory recall and elevated state of mind, happiness, compassion. Tapped in and open to ideas and visions. In a coherent state of mind. To quote the late Wayne Dyer: **'We don't manifest what we want, we manifest what we are.'**

Ways to get into a coherent state and to be the best that you can be; welcome to the elevator technique. Put both of your feet on the floor. A lot of times we live with our legs crossed. If our feet aren't on the ground, we're physically and energetically ungrounded. So, with your feet on the floor, close your eyes. Eighty percent of our sensory information comes in through the eyes. Close them, the brain starts to quiet down. Just take a deep breath, keep your eyes closed, sit comfortably. If you're holding tension anywhere, just kind of let that go. You are going down into the heart to see if there's something else that you need for your life right now. I want you to focus on yourself. Your life knows you best. Know what you need to hear. With your eyes closed, make yourself really small and go into an elevator which is in your mind. Just walk into the elevator.

It's not a typical office elevator. This is your elevator, imagine whatever you love and want in your elevator. Walk into your elevator and close the door. There are just two buttons. There's the M for the mind and an H for the heart. Hit the button H – just breathe. Imagine that elevator slowly leaving your mind, traveling down past your eyes, past your lips, your jaw, down your throat and neck, and down into your heart. As you visualize that, breathe from your heart space. Not lungs breathing, breathing from your heart. Let that elevator go all the way down to the heart and open the doors and walk out, watch your heart beating. Sit down next to your heart, get comfortable. You are going to stay here. Your heart has been beating since before you were born, and your heart is so powerful that you can hear it, and it's so strong you can feel it. Remember your breathing, just slowing down so that your heart and mind can sync, and pick an emotion that you would like to feel right now. Maybe your heart wants to feel something.

If the elevator tries to go back up into your mind, just get back in and slowly bring it back down to your heart. Your heart has probably been meaning to tell you something for a long time – wholeness, gratitude, relief, love. What is it your heart wants to tell you about your life right now? Just listen. What does your heart need to say? What did it notice about you that you need to hear? Where does your heart want to go? What does your heart want to be doing today? If your heart could kind of design the day, what would it be doing? Your heart has all the wisdom, it has all your truth. Scientifically, they've shown that your heart sends more signals off to the mind than the mind sends down to the heart.

Imagine all the signals that your mind would receive if you listened to your heart a little each day. Your heart and mind could be a powerful team, especially through the challenges. Make sure to capture what your heart needs to tell you, now that you've taken a moment to relax next to it. Just listen.

The mind is so limited, it's a record of the past. All it knows is what you read, what you listen to, the experiences you've had in the past. Oftentimes we're trying to chart our next steps in life by looking backwards. That's not how you get to where you really want to go. You've got to step into the unknown. I know every time I've ever had to make decisions that mattered, I've never been thinking about it, I listen to my heart.

Don't be logical in moments that are going to change your life, go into the heart and ask, 'Do I want this? How does it feel? Does this feel good? Is it exciting?' I always tend to make the call with the heart and then my mind. Our minds are amazing, but they're supposed to take directions from your heart.

The mind is louder and means you overthink things. It's like the mind is trying to sabotage the heart, like it doesn't want you to trust your heart.

We've over-trusted our minds too much. When we start to hear things from our heart, we might hear things that we don't want to hear. There's no proof that the heart is right, you have to start to trust yourself to do it. If you're overthinking, take the elevator down to your heart, and tell your mind 'I'll come back to you later'.

In the psychology of Carl Jung, an archetype is an inherited pattern of thought derived from the past experience of the whole race, which is present in our unconscious minds. We all have twelve archetypes; every person on the planet has the Saboteur archetype, which is essentially the habit of sabotaging ourselves by messing up our lives and relationships. And the Prostitute archetype, which engages lessons in the sale or negotiation of one's integrity or spirit due to fears of physical survival or for financial gain. We prostitute ourselves when we sell our bodies or minds for money or when we compromise our morals and ethics for financial gain.

Connecting your mind and heart will allow you to stop the sabotage, create alignment, and allow for refined self-esteem and self-respect.

How did you get yourself into a coherent state of mind?

I'm a big proponent of exercise, and sleep. I do my best to live in a more elevated state of emotion. I don't read the news. I decide what comes into my world rather than being affected by things coming at me. I'm choosing to do the elevator exercise because I know with the heart-mind coherence, that's where all the power is, that's where everything happens.

Where does the ego speak from, the mind or the heart? Always in the mind, as it's focused on survival. Our ego is solely focused on external things – money, power, fame, influence. The egos fear things. The heart might say, I really want to be a musician, and live my life in music to make money. The ego will say, That's not possible. You've got to go the traditional route or stay in banking, it's safer. Deep down, you might feel a rumbling. The rumbling isn't the ego, it's the other voice. It's your soul. The soul is in the heart, your spirit. I don't mean religion. I just mean the soul. The ego is never satisfied. It always wants more.

The power of intention was clear in a story about Oprah Winfrey. She had a mother come on the show to do an interview. The mother's sixteen-year-old daughter had been murdered by her boyfriend. She brought the woman into her office, and she said, 'Thank you for being here. What's the real reason you said yes? Why are we about to go and have this conversation? What do you want? What's your intention for being here?' And the mother said, 'My intention is not to talk about how my daughter was murdered by her boyfriend, it's to share that she had a life. And if there's one girl being abused by her boyfriend, she'll watch the show, and feel empowered to leave the guy. I just want to talk to those girls to get out of bad relationships.' And Oprah said, 'Let me help you with your intention. You need to talk to your mind and heart to tease out your intentions so that both can be aligned with the intention of making sure that that happens.'

We don't manifest what we want, we manifest what we are. When you squeeze an orange, orange juice comes out because that's what's inside. When you are squeezed, what comes out is what's inside. Squeeze yourself right now – what would come out? That helps me to make a choice or conscious choice of how I want to respond."

- TRACEY LIV

You can reach Tracey at *livlitceo.com*

As we headed for the weekend, I reflected on an unbelievably powerful week. We learned about branding, kindness, diet, adventure, and belief. And then to end it with peace and love was just magical. The talks were coming fast over the next couple of weeks, Chris Voss and Jordan Belfort were coming to talk to our team! Everyone was excited.

30

UPPING YOUR ELVIS

MAY 18, 2020

A conversation with
CHRIS BARÉZ-BROWN

CHRIS BARÉZ-BROWN IS A MASTER of transformation. He is fascinated by people and what makes them tick. By teaching people how to think differently, he makes their lives and businesses more technicolor. Chris was recently described by The Guardian as a "long-haired, twinkly-eyed cross between Richard Branson and a wizard." He talked about 'Upping your Elvis' so what did he mean by this?

"Upping your Elvis is understanding that regardless of what happens it will be an incredible day, even if the coffee runs out!...

It's about the energy we carry. When we tune up our energy, we have more success and more smiles. This isn't about having a cookie-cutter approach to energy. Find what works for you. Be a positive deviant, have fun and do better work, try things out, take it for the opportunity it is. Come back and be dangerous. Have fun and go on with your day. Focus on stuff that counts, not stuff that shouts for your attention. Recalibrate, come back, and continue; think, create, research, experiment, and adapt to your way of working.

How do we tune into that energy?

You can break down energy into four main components:

PHYSICAL ENERGY

It's not a badge of honor to ignore your physical energy. If you do, you are working on tasks with less energy than you require. Sleep research shows that top performers get 8.5 hours' sleep a day. We need to work on getting better sleep. Sleep early, be habitual on the time you go to sleep. We are not designed for monophonic sleeping, meaning that in a day there are two distinct periods: one for sleeping and one for wakefulness. We are designed for multi-sleep; napping is key, twenty minutes here and there.

Nutrition. Intermittent fasting, twelve to sixteen hours, not eating gives you an energy boost.

Movement – stand up, more people die from a sedentary lifestyle than from cigarettes and alcohol, it's important for focus as well.

One year with no beer. Removing alcohol elevates energy.

MENTAL ENERGY

We don't have great focus. The brain has not developed very much in fifty thousand years. We are scanning the horizon constantly for dangers. In the 21st century, those dangers are now problems, and we look out for them specifically. We can only be in deep focus for ninety minutes to two hours a day. Use that time when it counts.

We have a negativity bias. We learn from, and use, negative information far more than positive information. Negative events elicit more rapid and prominent responses than non-negative events. We recall and think about insults more than compliments, dwell on unpleasant or traumatic events more than pleasant ones, and focus our attention more quickly on negative rather than positive information. It's an autopilot to habitual patterns which saves energy. Move from this autopilot, plan to do different things and activities every day to break your bad habits.

Get a new stimulus into your life and avoid distraction from the outside world. Between 11am and 4pm, I have a mental 'Do not disturb' sign so I can focus on what is important.

EMOTIONAL ENERGY

Seventy percent of our energy is inspired by emotions. Embrace emotions. Unless they are embraced and expressed, they will come out in a way you don't want.

Walk and talk with people.

SPIRITUAL ENERGY

Live by your values. What feels right to you? Connect to your purpose, to the purpose of the company, have a meaning: why are you here on this planet? What drives you? Ask yourselves, what is my meaning and purpose? What is really important to me? Have intention to live by that every day. Make connections and connect what you do to bigger things. Loneliness is a problem in current society. We are developed to live in tribes and when we are not, our body reacts in a fight or flight response. If we don't have thirty-eight informal communications a week, our energy suffers. Phone somebody randomly each day, and ask: how are you? What is going on for you?

I go to the bottom of WhatsApp every week and text the

person I haven't spoken to in a while. It's a great habit.

Being in control from the moment you wake. Create routines, the first ninety minutes are the most important. When you wake, don't look at anything digital, drink water with a pinch of sea salt, exercise, sit quietly for a few minutes, focusing about your day – what is your intention for it? What do you want to deliver today?

Ask yourself every day:

- What three reasons am I excited for the day?
- What three reasons do I have to be grateful?
- Have I set today up to be the best day?
- How am I choosing to be today?"

- CHRIS BARÉZ-BROWN

You can reach Chris at *barez-brown.com*

I started texting the person at the bottom of my text and Whatsapp it really surprised me with lovely responses. This is your time to be different to everyone else and really stand out.

31

WE WERE HUNGRY LIKE THE WOLF

MAY 20, 2020

A conversation with
JORDAN BELFORT

I WONDER IF JORDAN agreed to do this because I cold called him. Maybe he liked the chutzpah of me. Who was this calling me at 8am on a Sunday morning? Whatever it was, it worked, and this was the one the team had been asking for. 'Please can you get The Wolf of Wall Street?' I delivered. As this was speech number twenty-three, we had already absorbed lots of information. This was a conversation about sales and life.

Jordan is a comeback king. At times of great adversity, the greatest opportunities present themselves. He shared ideas that we can use for our comeback, post-Covid.

"People in crisis get paralyzed, they get overtaken by fear, uncertainty, insecurity, and they end up doing nothing. Many people will use this as an excuse and they won't take any risks, and therefore accept a life of mediocrity and stay as it is, or probably get worse...

People close to me would say, 'If you flush Jordan down the toilet, he will come out holding a plumber's license.' I always have a way of somehow making things work. When I was seven years old, I was out knocking on doors; when I was ten years old, I was shoveling driveways after snowstorms to make money; and at the age of sixteen, I was going to the beach selling ice cream.

I'm scared shitless. I just don't let it stop me. I'm courageous. The point is, there's something about the way I go about seeing life and seeing business's success. It's not just unique to me, there are many people like me.

I'm not fearless, I do have fear, I just do not allow my fears to stop me from moving forward. That's the most important thing.

When I went to Wall Street, it was the end of the major five-year bull run. On my first day, just like you saw in the movie, the market crashed, and everybody back then believed it was the end, the next great depression. You know, blood on the streets, traders becoming cab drivers. I will never forget that day; I went home on the bus, I had no money, I was broke. And I remember that you could have heard a pin drop all over the city. Over those next few months, most people did nothing. If you look back now at that time, the greatest fortunes were made in those years following it, including mine.

So, consider this, every single time that there's a reset, something happens. There's a shakeup, and what happens is most people will live in a state of fear and uncertainty and do nothing. The reality is that now is the time to take massive action; it's still not too late.

How fast are you running now? In normal times everyone is running at the same pace. Right now, most of the people are on pause. This is your opportunity.

What I achieved in the first ninety days of Covid would have taken three years to have accomplished before.

There is always a path forward.

I have a definition of the 'inner world' of success, your success mindset, what goes on in your head before you take action.

The four elements of the inner world of success:

If you have these qualities you will succeed, you won't be able to help yourself.

STATE MANAGEMENT – managing your emotions – how you show up in the moment is the most important. You can have all the skills in the world; if your mindset is poor, then, you can't close a fucking door. You have to be in an empowered state.

YOUR BELIEF SYSTEMS – there are certain beliefs that we have that lead people to massive success, and there are other beliefs that lead them to failure, misery, and feeling alone. One of my beliefs is that in times of crisis, I can make money. I'm not a creature of circumstance, I make my own luck and fortunes.

VISION FOCUS – you have to create a vision for your future, and then learn how to focus on that vision in a way that allows you to move towards it, not with tunnel vision, but scanning the horizon for opportunities along the way. You need to identify your why, why do you want this success? And if you don't have your why, you're not going to be motivated; you have to be able to get yourself to do the things you have to do each day, even when you don't feel like doing them. That's the key rule for success. It's about mastering the art of doing what you hate to get what you love. You cannot have a champagne vision and beer standards.

YOUR PERSONAL STANDARDS – what level of success do you hold yourself to? What will you not settle for less than? I will not stop, I will not rest, unless I have X amount of dollars, X amount of success, X level of business. I won't stop until I have a loving, great marriage. I will manage my diet and my health until I am where I want to be. All success starts in your brain.

And there's an 'outer world' of success. This consists of the following:

THINK LIKE A BUSINESS PERSON – think entrepreneurially and have a plan. Start your own business and know the rules. Sell something. Marketing, market yourself on all the media outlets, and market yourself to attract the right people, and have MSI – multiple streams of income. What do you do with the money once you make it? How do you make money out of money? If you want to be rich, start your own business or be a salesperson. You don't need all the risks to be rich, find a great product and sell it. Make sure you understand every way to reach your audience.

SKILL UP – learn every aspect of it. People who want to do well are investing in themselves.

BE CAREFUL WHERE YOU WORK – Turn up trained. The first thirty days of your sales career are the most important. Learn like a scholar, especially at the beginning of your career, and make sure you know what you need to know before you start.

I use a technique called olfactory anchoring to elicit a positive internal response to an external trigger. Richard Bandler (the founder of NLP) developed it and I learned it from him. Use your sense of smell to get you into the right state of mind. Whenever I close a deal and feel the rush of success, I pull out my trusty essential oil inhaler, and take a big whiff, anchoring in the peak emotional state. Then, whenever I need an extra boost of confidence, I take it out and do the same, recalling the peak state and instantly flooding my body with confidence!

Who inspires you?

Buffett, Bezos, Musk, and Branson – they are examples of self-belief. And you have to understand where they came from, what hurdles they overcame to achieve greatness.

Other tips for success: create a script, making sure that it is actually written in a way that allows you to follow. It's gotta be you, it's got to flow in a certain manner that people will trust and believe, not sound like you are reading a script; you have to sound natural and use it. It's all about repetition, drilling, repetition.

Does money drive happiness?

Look, I've been rich and I've been really, really happy. I have been rich and I've been miserable too. I've been poor and I've been miserable. Money doesn't buy happiness, but a lack of money is a world of misery. Nothing sucks like poverty. Unless I'm making ten million dollars plus a year, I am miserable inside. I am not happy, I'm conflicted. Now does that mean I always made more than ten million dollars a year? No, it doesn't. But what it does mean is I will not settle for less. I'll keep going, I'll keep working, and things have turned out okay."

- JORDAN BELFORT

Jordan answered so many questions about the movie, life, and gave the team a free training session. My son Zac asked Jordan what the best advice to be a great salesperson was. He said, "Average Sucks." He definitely left us energized and engaged.

Six months after this talk, I was in the Den (Jordan's podcast), talking about the business and what we had been through. His intro to that podcast was probably one of the reasons I kept going. The last thing he told me as I was leaving his home was, "I will back you to survive." How could I let either of us down?

Follow Jordan Belfort on all social media *@wolfofwallst*

32

MEET THE KING OF SERENDIPITY

MAY 21, 2020

A conversation with
HOWARD LEWIS

AFTER THE ENERGY of the wolf, it was time to slow down and focus on the team's emotional wellbeing. I asked my dear friend Howard Lewis to kick this stage off.

A cultured man about town, Howard is incredibly creative and curious, and brings a multifarious box of tricks to the table. He is the king of serendipity and brings people together to see what happens. I was one of those people many moons ago. He and I remained friends. He is an art dealer and keeps threatening to educate me about art.

Howard came to talk about his thinking behind OFFLINE. The fundamental premise behind it was that in a wired world people needed more than ever to engage in physical interaction with one another. OFFLINE is designed to be the antithesis of everything online and recognizes that veering off-road and then back on it is both valuable and necessary. It aims to challenge and provoke, question and answer, stimulate and amuse, nurture, and nourish in a delightful and congenial setting.

"We are all born with one remarkable gift that no animal possesses, that gift is smiling...

The problem we have is that we are too concerned about the way we're perceived. We treat life as a competition and we overcomplicate things; simplicity is life's greatest virtue. Find a way to do things in a simple and uncomplicated way. In all physical interaction we need to demonstrate our humanity, take pleasure in sharing other people's pleasure, and think about how you make people feel about themselves. It's all about doing things from the goodness of our hearts. Just turn up and be the best version of yourselves. Be interested in people, find points of convergence – things in common. Be curious. It's about the value you can add. Ask yourself after the interaction: who are you going to be after this? How can you be a nicer human being? I went to an exhibition which I didn't really want to go to, just to show up and support my friend. We need to stop being so self-absorbed in our own lives and celebrate and support others.

Give and give. Listen, people don't listen enough. We have two ears and one mouth for a reason.

In a world where we are continuously bombarded by drama, people are really scared. It's about how we treat others which gives them confidence and reduces fear. Go to a museum with other people, eat with people; you will be surprised about the serendipities in life. Find common ground, find time in the office to connect with others. Food is a great way to bring people together, break the ice, and express a universal truth. Do you fart in bed? Allow yourself to fail. Give people permission to be vulnerable.

Be positive, come with a smile, it's about being aware that there is far more in life that connects us than separates us. It's so important to reinforce those things that connect us. Have a positive frame of mind, extend your hand physically and metaphorically. Be open, warm, and more importantly, listen. A quick tip on how to improve your listening is to read more books, slow down, and be patient."

- HOWARD LEWIS

Reach Howard at *@offlinehoward* on Twitter.

33

WHAT'S ON YOUR LIST?

MAY 27, 2020

A conversation with
SEB TERRY

SEB WAS SUPPOSED to turn up the day before – as we all sat and waited patiently, he didn't show. We used it as an opportunity to discuss what we learned so far. The feedback was great, and the guys were inspired. We watched a video Seb had sent, and we all decided to make our list of the 100 things we wanted to do. Obviously I overdelivered and did ten more.

Seb was devastated he missed the chat, and we agreed to do it the next day.

I had shared my list with the group and Seb. One thing on mine was to read poetry out loud, so Seb challenged me to write a poem and read it to the group. It was a wonderful experience and a little mic drop moment. In five minutes, I talked about all the speakers and what we learned in rhyme. I wonder if this might have been the inspiration for me to start writing poems?

The guys were looking forward to his chat. Seb told us his story: an ordinary Australian guy with a weird list which has now grown into a beautiful, organic community of people around the world, who are all dreamers – and doers!

> "I went down the usual college route, followed the path that was put in front of me, and I still didn't feel great. My reaction was to go backpacking overseas with no money, darting around from country to country, continent to continent, but with no real direction...
>
> Suddenly, one night, I got a phone call from a friend in Australia to tell me one of his close friends growing up, Chris – who he went to school with, played rugby with, drank with, who was a pivotal character in his life – had passed away very suddenly and very tragically.
>
> It made me think life is way too short, but when I thought of Chris, he was really fortunate that he was able to live in a

BY SIMON LESLIE   A conversation with **SEB TERRY**   241

way that reflected his values. As I sat in Canada at the age of twenty-four, I asked myself, in this moment, the middle of the night, if today was my last, would I be happy? I had never looked at his own life with that perspective and, almost instantly, realized I would change everything. It wasn't that I was depressed or anything like that, I just had no purpose. I just didn't know who I was and didn't know my values. In that moment I realized I was unhappy. That was the thought behind creating the list, to do things that would make me happy.

I'm not a psychologist. But I do think when people hit rock bottom, they have this propensity, which is beautiful, by default to push off the bottom and try and do whatever it is for us to rise. Why wait till you hit rock bottom? Give yourself permission to consider what else is there for you, and then choose to pursue that, just do it. Go, you'll never know whether it's right until you do something. Your goals should stem from values, and when they do, you don't get bored, you don't lose motivation, because you understand the other things make you live well, be happy and smile. Be a better father or brother or mother or sister or friend or colleague or supplier or client or customer.

So, I thought, I'm going to prioritize my happiness. And that was the beginning of the list. I got a pen and a piece of paper and just began jotting down things that I thought would make me smile and would bring me closer to a sense of happiness.

Did you know that when you write a goal down, you become eighty-three percent more likely to achieve it. Once you put something down on paper in front of you, you become very focused on it, and it engages a problem-solving machine – how can I? How can I solve it - starts the brain on a journey, to make those beautiful, wonderful things start to happen? There was never any thought other than I'm just going to try and be happy. I'm breathing, I'm alive. I have therefore an opportunity to change something. And I just began creating the list; ten became twenty and then there was a list of a hundred things.

I used to never do anything because I didn't want to fail, I didn't want to seem silly. I used to really care about what people would say, I'd get nervous, all the time. These stopped me, I'd just walk away. I still have all those feelings; I just process them differently.

I say to myself now, 'This is a really good opportunity for me to step forward'. Imagine a triangle, the top is belief, one of the corners to the right is action. On the left-hand side is the result. Your belief clearly influences your action, and your action directly your result. And the result will again go on to reinforce your belief. So, if you're a negative person who's pessimistic, the world's not fair, you know, it's a horrible and cruel world. If that's your belief, you will make nothing happen.

You can't control the environment all the time, but you can control your response. As an example, take this call; we could all be sitting on our hands and wait till Covid is over and everything opens up. But no, we took it upon ourselves to connect, so you controlled your response.

Imagine, if you're on your deathbed, and you're lucky enough to have a moment to consider your life, looking back at everything you've done, will you have regrets or wish you did things differently? Don't wait for a bad event. Don't wait for someone to lose their life next year. Don't wait to get diagnosed with an illness. Start doing it today, it doesn't need to cost huge amounts of money, sometimes it just needs creative thinking.

I've done seventy-four things from the original list. There's never been a plan or design. It's just sort of worked organically. And I keep finding out every single day that people want to connect. We need to be ready when those opportunities present themselves. On my list is to catch a thief, I don't know when that's going to happen. You can't plan everything, so be ready for the opportunity. The way to respond to an opportunity is just knowing in the first place what you need, what your goal is, what is it you want to do? And then what are the opportunities you need to create? Or what are the opportunities you need to just wait for?

Opportunities come when we look at sharing and being a community. A community of like-minded go-getters inspiring others. If I can share my and their story with my community, someone out there will be able to help. As an example, there was a guy in Oregon, he wanted to build a treehouse in memory of his son and for other kids to enjoy. He didn't know how to build a treehouse. He shared his story, and over three days, twenty people from around the US flew to Oregon to help him build it. Why? Because people are good, because that's actually what matters. None of this materialistic stuff, we just want to be a service and actually connect with each other. And be accountable for each other.

I met Mark, a quadriplegic man from Melbourne, Australia. He was the victim of a tick bite which infected him with Lyme disease. He lost the ability to move and speak. After hearing of the 100 things, Mark approached me and asked me to help him achieve his dream of completing a half marathon – he just needed someone to push him. This moment allowed me an opportunity to help someone with their own list for the first time, and so I immediately said yes. To this day, helping push Mark across the finish line of the half marathon remains one of the greatest accomplishments of my life, and I haven't stopped helping people since.

I did a workshop with a bank. And when everyone shared their goals, people said, I want to go hang gliding, run a marathon etc., and then the CEO stood up and said, 'I want to hug my dad,' in tears, and everyone else started crying.

Anything is possible, and here are a few items I have

achieved on my list. Marry a stranger. I went straight to Las Vegas and married a stranger. It was a very bizarre experience. I met a stripper, an exotic dancer called Crystal, in a ball of mud, and I proposed to her. I was very honest and open, and she said, 'Yeah, I'll marry you'. I booked this drive-through wedding chapel to say I do, and she stood me up. There were twenty people in the chapel, and I didn't know any of them. So when I made a plea to the crowd, 'Is there anyone here who'd like to marry me?' One of those people, it turns out, had always wanted to marry someone, too. She said yes. I remember feeling instantly in control of my life. I felt empowered, and I think it was because up until that point in my life, I had never been in control and given myself permission to be happy.

Another item on my list was I wanted to get shot! And I wondered what the best way was. I googled bulletproof clothing companies, and a company in Colombia popped up. They make bulletproof body suits. I emailed the owner of the company and said, 'Would you mind shooting me?' And he said, 'Yeah, no worries, just come to Bogota'. So, I did, and I ended up getting shot. I saw him squeeze the trigger, and although I was really confident that nothing would go wrong, I remember at that moment thinking, What if it does? What if I die now? But if I die now, will I die happy? I just realized I actually would.

At the age of thirty-two, a friend of mine was diagnosed with late-stage aggressive cancer and was given six months.

On the way home, he decided that rather than calling people to say goodbye and being in bed, waiting to die, he would do the one thing that he'd always wanted to do: go on a global shopping spree. He went to four different banks, somehow got four different credit cards, and a week later, he left on a global shopping spree everywhere around the world: Tokyo, Milan, London, Paris, to name a few places. He accumulated debt on these credit cards of ninety thousand US dollars. He had everything; he had suits, shoes, watches, and you know, all the things. The funny part of the story is he is still alive thirty years on. And when he told me the story, I thought, *Oh, my God what an idiot.*

'Do you regret what you did?' I asked him, and he said, without a moment's hesitation, 'No, I don't regret it. The moment I was told that my life was in jeopardy, it was the first moment I gave myself permission to consider my own version of happiness'."

- SEB TERRY

Connect with Seb at *@seb100things* on social media.

Before the talk I decided to compile my list, it's funny now, how few I have completed, I need to focus more. This book is number 40.

My 100 list

1. Watch my horse win a race
2. Take a team back to Lapland
3. Go to Bora Bora
4. Go to Fiji
5. Take a team to Machu Picchu
6. Skydive
7. Mentor 7 under 20s
8. Build a school – physically in Africa
9. Go to Columbia
10. Visit Peru
11. Go to Uruguay
12. Raise $50,000 from No F In Sales Book sales
13. Drive a camper-van across America
14. Take the wife to NZ
15. Learn Spanish
16. Dive with Great white sharks
17. Take an Ink team to the South Pole
18. Have a conversation with Jeff Bezos
19. Have coffee with Elon Musk
20. Go to Necker Island
21. Play soccer at the Emirates Stadium
22. Play soccer at Inter Miami
23. Coach a football manager
24. Meet Simone Leslie
25. Go to Lithuania and see where my namesake was born

26. Speak to 1000+ people
27. Appear on a soap opera
28. Be in a movie
29. Buy 100 meals for homeless people
30. Write a poem and recite it publicly
31. Live for 24 hours in silence
32. Go to a detox retreat for a month
33. Walk 100k London to Brighton
34. Cycle from London to Brighton
35. Cycle from Brighton to Bournemouth
36. Play roulette with Benjy in Vegas
37. Go to the Taj Mahal
38. Coach 5 new people
39. Be in a show
40. Write a lockdown book
41. Create a podcast
42. Go to Pray in 20 countries
43. Play tennis with a top 100 player.
44. Play top ten golf course
45. Help a complete stranger
46. Break a world record
47. Go to a football game in Columbia
48. Crash a wedding
49. Throw a superb 2021 party of the year
50. Go on CNBC
51. Go on Bloomberg

52. Write 52 handwritten letters
53. Help a professional football manager
54. Go to a fortune teller
55. Smoke Cuban with a Cuban
56. Go to the Arc de Triomphe race
57. Watch the full moon in Goa
58. Go the long way to Tipperary
59. Be a cowboy in Montana
60. Camp out Safari
61. Go to the gorillas in Rwanda
62. Gamble at Genting in the cloud in Malaysia
63. Go in the sea in Brighton in December
64. Do something for a homeless person
65. Stay in a lodge in Inverness
66. Play tennis at flushing meadow
67. Pick up a hitchhiker
68. Learn to make a cocktail
69. Go to Boracay
70. Avoid clothes for a week
71. Go dog sledding in Alaska
72. Be vegan for three months
73. See the salt lakes in Bolivia
74. Visit Petra
75. Take Natalie to Galapogos
76. See the cherry blossom in Japan
77. Take Natalie to Osaka
78. Sleep in an igloo

79. Make my own bottle of wine
80. Go to the pyramids
81. Sail down a Norwegian Fjord
82. Volunteer at an orphanage
83. Sleep in a tree house
84. Drive route 66
85. See an opera at Met in NY
86. Spend time with the Masi Mara tribe
87. Have a mud bath in Palau
88. Name a star after me
89. Walk to work
90. Go to the cinema during a work day
91. Buy 5 strangers coffee (pay it forward)
92. Pay for someone dinner in a restaurant
93. Perform magic tricks
94. Join the mile high club
95. Do a tandem bike ride
96. Run a race with Natalie
97. Have a cream tea together
98. Eat pasta in the Amalfi coast
99. Eat Paella in Ibiza with Natalie
100. Take Natalie to the Algarve
101. Shower in a waterfall
102. Spend an afternoon reading in the NY central Library
103. Spend a morning in the British Library
104. Sail around the Greek islands

105. Walk around a city all night long
106. Have a pair of shoes made
107. Have a suit made when I lose four stone
108. Do something that scares me
109. Take Zac to the Louvre
110. Watch Scott play football at a professional club

34

NEGOTIATING WITH THE BEST

28 MAY, 2020

A conversation with
CHRIS VOSS

IT'S EARLY IN VEGAS, yet when Chris' calming voice came through the Zoom room it was like being transported to a place of zen. As with everything to do with Chris, it was intentional, practiced, and based on neuroscience. It's not a surprise that he was the lead international kidnaping negotiator for the FBI and his Masterclass on negotiation is now one of the most successful on the market. If we think negotiating a monetary deal is tough, just imagine what it must be like to negotiate in a life-or-death situation. The pressure of getting it wrong with extreme consequences, now that's real pressure. And, as I have always said, pressure is a privilege.

"After twenty-four years with the Bureau, I left and set up The Black Swan Group to train negotiation. I also made time to teach business negotiation at Harvard, and to guest lecture at The Kellogg School of Management at Northwestern University, the IMD Business School in Lausanne, Switzerland, and the Goethe Business School in Frankfurt, Germany...

When I started on my journey as a negotiator, the skills and behaviors required were often seen as a dark art – more voodoo than science. When the scientific community took an interest all of a sudden, it had a title, 'the act of labeling emotions', and today we refer to it as neuroscience.

So, what bits of neuroscience do we need to know? We all have a limbic system – and it controls our emotions. It's wired to work the same way for everyone. The limbic system comprises four parts, one of which is the amygdala. The amygdala is a gateway where all our emotions flow (did you know we have around 38,400 emotions?). From research of brain activity, from measuring how the brain patterns flow and light up as a result, seventy-five percent of our emotions are negative – it's all based on science. When people are shown negative images – war, death, or hardships – they have negative emotions, it lights up in the limbic system. If then they start to talk about that negative emotion, then the lights reduce. The negative activity in the limbic system reduces. The lesson here is if we talk about the negative emotion then that emotion diminishes. A bit scientific, but it will all make sense shortly.

As negotiators, all we ever hear are negative emotions – after all, what can you say to someone holding hostages at a bank? One tactic I learned early on was that by listening and labeling that emotion as negative, and then calling out that emotion, then these negative emotions went away. You may think this is insane, (yes, I am using the technique now), but we must always call out the negative first, so that emotion goes away. People will never make a decision until you get rid of that negativity, as their brain shuts down.

We also need to have 'tactical empathy', and empathy isn't always truthful and honest. It can reflect the fears people have, and using tactical empathy, we get people thinking about those fears. It is important to understand that people are more motivated away from loss, rather than towards gain. And that's the most important thing to remember during a negotiation.

To not blind us with science, I simply call it, 'The elephant in the room'. We need to get that negative emotion, negative perceptions out at the beginning – get the elephant in the room out first, before we can move on. By calling out the negative, people will want to help you.

Here are some examples of the elephant in the room in practical terms:

If you want someone to try a new product, you can say to them, 'You are probably scared about trying something new?'

When you want to create urgency, 'I want you to think about what's going to happen if you don't make the move, what's going happen if you don't deal with the issue you arrived with today. If you don't take action, you're still going to be dealing with it when you wake up in the morning'.

Try it when you want an upgrade on a room in a hotel. Walk up to the front desk and say to the receptionist, 'I am going to ruin your day' – and watch the receptionist process the seventy-five percent negative limbic emotion. OMG, has he got body parts in his bag, is he incontinent, and what the hell is going to happen? Then build rapport and keep calling out the elephant. 'I don't want to come off as just another cheap traveler wanting something for nothing, I do appreciate the work that you guys do'. The next part is about tactical empathy and seeing things from their point of view. If he or she gives me this free upgrade, they are going to worry about getting in trouble. They are going to worry about people being mad. So then say, 'how do I get a free upgrade to one of your hotel suites without pissing everybody in the hotel off?'

Another story I use to illustrate this point was a business example from a friend and company owner called Robin. She had an events business and as the pandemic hit was due to lose $1.8m of revenue, and she was desperately panicking about her business's survival, she asked me for advice – 'It's going to wipe me out', she said, 'I am not sure we are going to survive, what should I do?'

I shared the elephant in the room concept and told her to call the negative out. 'You say to them exactly what you just said to me. Say this is a shit show. You are worried about whether or not you're gonna survive. You're worried about whether or not you're going to be able to make payroll, you're scared to death. You don't know what's going to happen. And then say to them, how do we work our way through this together so that we don't destroy each other? And we leave ourselves in a position to thrive together when this is over'.

You will notice, from the last two examples, that after calling out the elephant in the room, I asked a question. It's not a question to get information, it's what I call a 'thought-provoking question'. These are questions to get someone to think rather than to gain information – how do we work our way through this? You plant thoughts in their heads.

A thought-provoking question in a terrorist negotiation could be, 'how do we work our way through this so that we don't destroy each other, and we leave ourselves in a position to be successful together?' You can also call out the fear, but not as a threat. 'You know, I'm not the threat in this situation. And your best way through this threat is by collaborating with me'.

A story that you can all use at some point in the future is the story of a young salesman who was new to a business and selling much more than his experienced colleagues. He went to his boss one day and said that he wanted a raise. His boss said that it would not be fair on people who had been there for a longer time. The boss said, 'Tell you what, if you can come up with a way that I can give you a raise that's fair and equitable for everybody else, I'll do it,' and he gave the executive two weeks to come up with a plan. Two weeks later, the executive goes back to see the boss and says there is no way to do it which will be fair and equitable to everybody – he calls out the elephant in the room.

With tactical empathy, he says, 'But this isn't about fairness and equity. This is about what's best for the company'. The boss was given a way to work it out for himself and he ended up negotiating his compensation package.

There is nothing I like to do more than watch people. People give you lots of signals about what they are feeling and thinking, we just need to be observant and look more. He is sensitive to how they are walking, looking, standing, and their facial expressions. You get a massive amount of information about what is going through the person's mind at that moment.

I remember airline counter staff not smiling, and intentionally not making eye contact. So, I used my assessment, called out the negative and simply said in my late-night DJ voice, 'Tough day?' And she just gathered her thoughts once the negative had been called out and said, 'No. No. How can I help?' with a smile on her face. Did I get anything out of that? No, but she felt better in that moment, and then maybe that rubbed off on someone else. It also allowed me to practice, and even the best negotiators need to practice.

It's all about practice, and then even more practice. Most people hone their craft from an early age, and before long they have their ten thousand hours towards mastery. I practice and review everything I do. For example, my voice and his tonality – I record, listen, and look at the effect it has on people.

Originally, it was a bit of that old black magic that worked so well; I noticed that using this voice calmed people down. I had no idea why, then science came along; it was all about chemical reactions. We have mirror neurons, which do what the name says – they mirror the behavior and actions of others. As an example, when you smile, people smile back and you feel good. When the neurons in your brain are activated, chemicals are released in your body. It's about chemical changes in your body that are triggered by thoughts.

If I use the late-night DJ voice, that voice hits your mirror neurons, and it triggers a chemical change and chemicals get injected into your brain. If you simply downward inflect – and you don't just have to be a man to do this – it causes a chemical reaction in people's brains and calms them down. The first words out of your mouth are hitting their mirror neurons before you finish the sentence. You haven't even put together enough words for them to have any idea what you're talking about.

What does a negotiator know about features and benefits?

In negotiating, as in selling, we need to understand and get into the mind of what the person wants quickly, rather than throwing features and benefits around. What if the feature you give is important to you and not the buyer? Or it's third on their list? We need to get into their heads straight away, as people have short attention spans. So this is where we can use the good old 'thought provoking question'. Ask them: 'You must be here for a reason?', 'It seems like you have a reason for being here', and as we know, when a thought provoking question is used, then the answers just flow."

- CHRIS VOSS

I don't think I have the capacity to imagine the responsibility of having other people's lives depending on the words I use and my assessment of a situation. This, I guess, is where training, knowledge, and reliance on a process help. In our business negotiations it's not about life or death, it is about everyone feeling like they got the best deal. This can only be done if there is great communication.

During the pandemic, I was negotiating a major contract breakdown and using my notes from the call; with the help of a few more pointers from Chris, we settled what could have been a huge problem for the business, and turned it into a huge opportunity. So my commitment to Chris is to help him have his own TV show on our ReachTV network.

To connect with Chris, visit *blackswanltd.com*

35

JUNE 2020

WE ARE LOSING MONEY like water, no one is traveling, we are burning through cash, to keep everyone whole, and people are questioning whether there is going to be a business. Despite all of this, I feel alive and inspired by the speakers from May; the pictures in my mind of Carla walking up and down the steps to keep herself fit, while undergoing chemo, through to Voss and his late night DJ voice. Alison drudging through the snow, pulling the heavy load. My list of 100 things is a powerful reminder there is still so much to do in the world. And of all the English chaps, James Harris just seemed to be a brother from another mother. We have the same positive outlook on life, and this pandemic was not going to change that.

Reality has set in. The office once housed three hundred, but now there are only seven of us moping around, trying to find something to do. We close our NY office; they are all working from home anyway. The football season kicks off in Portugal and the first goal scorer is Jesus Corona – you can't make this shit up. I line up some more speakers for June and hope this will be over soon. Sports start again behind closed doors, but it's not the same. The Olympics are canceled for a year. Stores are still shut, protesting and marching continues through all the big cities across the world in support of Black Lives Matter. Loose reopening started towards the end of the month. No one wanted to be associated with travel at this point.

Michael and I are invited to talk to the business students at Oxford University Said Business School – a real honor. Here was I, who never went to school properly, let alone university, talking at one of the finest universities on the planet, and they were loving our story. I remember saying to the professor and Michael, "when we get out of this pickle, that will be a great story to tell the next group of students." Yes this book is on the way....

After months of hiding, we make a positive move, we decided to buy a small technology business, which we believe will give us an edge to get back on track, especially as many of the airlines don't see the magazines coming back this year, if at all. When people travel again, we will be able to target them at all parts of the passenger journey. I set us a target of $7.5 million for the second half of 2020 – that's a long way from the $75 million we had budgeted.

36

TIME FOR SOME STOICISM

JUNE 15, 2020

A conversation with
JONAS SALZGEBER

WHAT CAN SOMEONE from the third century BC teach us about life in the twenty-first century AD? The reality is, a lot. Okay, we have twenty-first century problems, yet the essence of life is still the same.

Early in June, we had Jonas Salzgeber come talk to us about his book, The Little Book of Stoicism: Timeless Wisdom to Gain Resilience, Confidence, and Calmness. I love Stoicism, I believe that so many of the lessons are still relevant today.

To quote Epictetus, a Greek Stoic philosopher, "How long are you going to wait before you demand the best for yourself?" And that's the essence of Stoicism. Stoic philosophy guides us through life – and we all need that at times. Jonas took us on his journey of discovery through his book. He wanted to share a simple, concise, and easy-to-understand message about how Stoic philosophy could help. He told us that he wasn't a professor, just a simple guy encouraging us to understand and, more importantly, bring it into our everyday lives.

"So, a quick guide to Stoicism...

What it's not, as most people think, is about suppressing our emotions. It's not about suppressing them, bottling them up, but it's about acknowledging the emotions and managing them. You are in control, it's about stepping back and asking how you want to respond in the present moment.

Stoicism is about living the good life, and we can achieve that by expressing our best self in every moment. What matters to the Stoics is not outward success, but who you are, the person behind the curtains. Stoicism is about being our best and expressing our best. We have to focus on what we can control, know the things we can't control, and take responsibility to be able to respond appropriately to a situation. It's about tranquility and peace of mind; this is achieved, the Stoics tell us, if our actions align with our values.

Think of Stoicism as a happiness triangle. In the center of the triangle is what we all hope for in our lives – a good life, being good, our higher self and flourishing. In each of the corners of the triangle are attitudes and behaviors to achieve it.

One of the corners is virtue, and to avoid any misinterpretations, I define virtue as expressing the best version of yourself, moment to moment.

The second corner is about making the best use of what is in our power. We should focus on the things we control and accept the things we don't control. Imagine, an archer; you have a bow and arrow, and you try to hit the target. Ask yourself, what's in my control? Preparation, practice, you can choose the bow and arrow, and in the moment you can focus. The moment you release the arrow, it is out there in the air. Maybe the wind is going to blow stronger, or the target is going to move, or something is going to step in between the arrow and the target. You cannot control that, so focus on the things you can control. Once the arrow is gone, reality is there and reality is neutral. It is our judgment that makes it good or bad.

The final corner is about taking responsibility. As a word, I'll break it down; it's response ability. It's our ability to respond. The difference between reaction and response. Response is the reaction that is always instigated by an outside stimulus. Something happens and we react to it automatically.

Before we react automatically we should pause, step back from our impulse or first impression and choose a response.

Things happen. It might look like an obstacle, a problem, or a challenge. If we just automatically react to it then we may not find the right answers. Marcus Aurelius said, 'What stands in the way, becomes the way'. To paraphrase Epictetus, if there weren't twelve challenges for Hercules, then Hercules would have just rolled over in bed, and he would never have developed into this mighty Hercules. We need the challenges and hurdles in life so we can grow. We should be ten feet tall by now with all the challenges we have faced so far.

Probably the most famous Stoic, Marcus Aurelius, one of the most powerful men of his time, was a Roman emperor in AD 143. He was a real humble guy. At the end of every day he would reflect on the day and write up his learnings in his journal. Like Marcus Aurelius, if we reflect on a daily basis, we grow more mindful throughout the day because we already know we are going to reflect upon these actions in the evening.

Ask yourself three questions:

- What did I do well today?
- What can I do better tomorrow or in the future?
- What could I do to make the most of the future?

The next technique I'll share is, taking the bird's eye view. Imagine you are somewhere above yourself. Look down at yourself to gain some perspective. With this new perspective, maybe the problem is not such a big deal.

For the Stoics, it was important to remind themselves of

the impermanence of nature. They said that nature changes and everything changes constantly. As they say in The Lion King – it's just another circle of life, for example, you know, you're born, and then there's life and then there's death. And we see nature all the time with animals and with plants and birds. So, it's normal that things change, and maybe that's where the beauty of nature can be found. It's changing nature.

Picture a blooming flower; if it bloomed all the time maybe it'd be less appreciated. So, it's important to remind ourselves of the impermanence of everything. It may be graying hair, that's just part of nature; you grow old. Understand there is no permanence, all the things we think we own, they are borrowed from nature.

For the Stoics, it was important to always keep on learning: 'You're a student of life, a lover of wisdom, someone who loves to learn'. External students, we need to be humble in our learning, we need to remain open-minded.

No matter what century we are in, we always look for meaning. Stoicism as a way of life gives us that meaning. It goes beyond a pandemic, and once we realize that we cannot control everything, and we can only control how we respond, this will give you a life of fulfillment and happiness."

– JONAS SALZGEBER

Jonas can be contacted at *njlifehacks.com*

37

THIS IS A TIME TO BE GRATEFUL

JUNE 16, 2020

A conversation with
CHESTER ELTON

SAT IN HIS ORANGE ATTIRE, Chester is known as the 'Apostle of Appreciation' and he fully deserves that title. He practices what he preaches – and he leads with gratitude every day. He is the gratitude man! It was like listening to a great man share his knowledge on a subject he was clearly so passionate about. The more speakers we listened to, it was clear many were fans of each other.

"I start my day with 'Thank you', and I end my day with 'Thank you', and I fill as much of my day in between with as many 'Thank yous' as I can...

I just find it is a better way to live and is a way of keeping in a positive mindset. We feel better, live longer, lower our blood pressure. We are happier, feel fulfilled, and achieve more when we practice gratitude every day. And by practicing it every day, you will be surrounded by positive people – after all, gratitude attracts gratitude.

We all suffer from the twenty-first century disease by spending all our time focusing on what we don't have rather than what we do, and this is dangerous. My father would say: 'Yesterday is history. Tomorrow is a mystery. Today is a gift. That's why they call it the present'.

I have two stories to share – a business story from Garry Ridge, CEO of WD-40, and an emotional story of the plight of children in Africa.

What does WD-40 stand for? Water Displacement, 40th formula – in their lab in San Diego, California, this was the experiment test number and the name just stuck – it took thirty-nine attempts to get the product right and on the fortieth it worked. And now in every household there is a can of WD-40. The WD-40 thinking was not that they failed thirty-nine times, it was that they had thirty-nine learning moments to get it right. 'Don't waste a good crisis,' Garry said. So, don't waste this pandemic.

Invest your energy, time and thinking into areas you can improve, personally and professionally.

Marshall Goldsmith, a friend of mine, travels a lot. And he said, 'You know, it's always interesting to me that people get so upset when traveling, about things over which they have absolutely no control'. When they announce that the airplane is going to be late, the usual group dynamic is of bitter complaints – Come on, how can you do this to me?

The reality of the situation is you can do nothing about it; you're not the pilot, you don't control the weather, you don't control the slots of the airport. When I feel like this, I remember a humanitarian trip I had to Africa for the Red Cross. We're with a whole bunch of children, and their arms are being measured. The reason we were measuring their arms is because if their arms were too big, we didn't give them food that day, they could survive without eating that day. If their arms measured too small, giving them food wouldn't matter, they were going to die. If their arms were just the right size, we gave them food. I wanted to remind myself that there are people in the world that have real problems we can't even imagine, like whether I'm going to be able to eat today or not. Whenever I feel justifiably upset, I think of those children; be grateful that the only thing that's going wrong for you today is your plane is late.

The chicken and egg dilemma.

Is it joy that makes us grateful or is it gratitude that makes us joyful? It's not joy that makes us grateful. It's gratitude that makes us joyful. I never think that what's coming is as bad as it really is, because I'm grateful to have so much, and that leads me to be joyful.

Gratitude journals are a great way to deal with stress and anxiety, and don't just take Chester's word for it. The University of California and University of Pennsylvania did studies on people that kept gratitude journals. It impacted them emotionally and intellectually; they found that they slept better, and their blood pressure was lower. They had more meaningful and deeper relationships with the people around them.

My father was a great man for journaling – in fact, that was his legacy. There is real value in reflecting.

Ask yourself four questions every day:

1. What did I set out to do today, what were my goals today?
2. What happened during that day?
3. What did I learn?
4. What am I going to carry forward from what I learned?

Plans never go as planned. As the famous philosopher Mike Tyson said, 'All the plans go out the window as soon as somebody punches you in the face'.

The most important words are intention and discipline. Be very intentional about the way you express gratitude and be very disciplined in that you do it every day.

I have a friend in Dallas, Texas, and one of the disciplines he has is to put ten coins in his pocket every day. And his goal would be to have ten positive interactions with the people. (We do this at Ink, it's about turning ten coins into thousands of dollars, every good conversation moves a coin.)

Another friend, who runs a social media advertising company in New York City, told me that when he is having a tough day, he takes a break, sets the timer on his phone for two minutes, and notes all the people that he is grateful for. By the end of two minutes, he feels better about himself.

We must always assume positive intent. When we interact with people, we often think and assume that there is negative intent. It's our way to protect and defend ourselves; we look for danger and we look for what's going wrong, as opposed to what's going right. When you assume positive intent, everything gets better.

Another friend changed the dynamic of his evening meal with his family. He made it a discipline that they all had to answer three questions.

You can also add these to your journal and ask them at the end of every day as well, it helps create a good end to he day:

- What was the best part of your day?
- Who are you grateful for that's not at the table?
- Who are you grateful for at the table that hasn't been thanked yet?

I had a friend (you would expect the Apostle of Appreciating to have many friends) give me a very simple breathing exercise. Hold your feet flat on the ground, straighten your back, breathe through your nose, exhale through your mouth, and do this for two minutes. It really helps during stressful times.

Prayer and meditation also help, taking the time for you to focus on what you have. It will give you strength to deal with the big things. Be disciplined, find thirty minutes a day to do it. Try it as well right before you go to bed, to change the mindset of all the negative news that comes through your phone and on TV – ninety percent of it is negative. Separate yourself from it, cheer yourself up.

Another technique – and not being morbid about it – is to picture yourself at your wake and think, what do you want people to be saying about you? And then live your life to achieve that story. Whilst gratitude is based on what you

> have now, there is no problem in creating what Chester calls a 'legacy', that is looking back, appreciating and being grateful for how far you've come. But don't get complacent, continue to strive, and then project: Where do you want to be? How do you want to get there? How can you get there in a way that your legacy will continue to be wonderful?"

> **- CHESTER ELTON**

Chester shared with the group his love of handwritten letters, as we have been at Ink for a long period of time. Handwritten notes are personal, and show that you care and have taken the time to write them. The great thing about a handwritten note is it's always timely, because when you get one, you make time to read it. Be disciplined with your intention to send them. Give yourself a number to send each week. We know there are different platforms to reach out to people, so use a combination of old and new.

Do this now – grab your smartphones, and I want you to text somebody, who in your mind you're grateful for. Maybe it's somebody in your family, maybe it's somebody you work for. Text them right now and make the message simple. I just want you to say 'I have just been thinking about you. I want to let you know how much you mean to me, how much I care about you,' and then sign off with, 'I love you'. I think right now more than ever, we're working from home or isolating. The big fear that we all have is being forgotten. These simple, little notes and these simple, little texts show you're not forgotten.

Chester shared some ideas and disciplines that he had discovered on his journey, to help us deal with the anxiety and stress of life by using gratitude to have a joyful life.

Call people, just call to check in and say, 'Just checking in. How are you doing today? How can I help?' And then listen. When there's a communication void, that void gets filled with rumor, innuendo and fear. When people don't call, the assumption is, they are not important, and you don't care. This is the same for business as in your personal life.

As a final summary, Chester said, "the more you do it, the better you'll get. And it'll go from being what you do to who you are. Stop the excuses for not being grateful; he told us a line from his father which I now use all the time. Excuses, even when valid, are never impressive."

Chester can be reached at *chesterelton.com*

Nothing is easier than saying 'thank you,' we all just need to do more of it. It's powerful beyond measure. Be grateful for what we have and celebrate it daily. And have a joyful life.

A few weeks after the talk, I was in a card shop and I saw a fluffy orange thank you card. I sent it to Chester, and he was delighted to receive it. It's my constant, consistent commitment to always do the right things.

38

TIME TO GO BIG

JUL 28, 2020

A conversation with
ALAN WATKINS

I SAW ALAN'S TED TALK, and I loved what he had to say, so I reached out and he kindly offered to help. When this is all over, I want to work closely with Alan, as I believe his work is incredible and he can take me to an even higher level.

A doctor for eleven years, Alan helps people understand emotional health. He loves to talk about the magic and tragic moments we all face in our lives, which are what makes us human and alive.

He shared with us two stories about men named Mike.

"Mike [1], had a meteoric rise in his medical career and, at a relatively young age, became a consultant – yet he was bored, terminally bored. He had reached the pinnacle of his career and didn't know what to do next...

Now Mike [2] had a different experience. He got his girlfriend pregnant at medical school, and by the time he qualified, he had three children. He wanted to 'let his hair down', and got a job in Saint Lucia, taking his family with him.

Getting there was a nightmare, with confusing travel arrangements which meant Mike [2] and his family arrived one week late, transported on a boat which nearly sank, and with three young children vomiting all the time. And on his arrival, he presented himself to the surgeon general, who said, 'As you were late, we didn't think you were coming,' and gave the job to someone else. 'But that's okay,' the surgeon said, 'we need an anesthetist so you can have that job'. Now, Mike [2] had no experience in being an anesthetist, so he read books to teach him all he needed to know. The thing with anesthetics is that once you put the patient to sleep, there is little to do. So, the surgeons operating asked Mike [2] to help with the operations. He did this for ten years and then got bored.

So he got a job as a flying doctor in Quebec and then returned to the UK. Looking for work in the UK, he was interviewed for a job as a consultant obstetrician. The professors interviewing commented that he didn't have the qualifications to do the job, so Mike [2] asked them, 'How many C sections have you done?' The professors thought that was not relevant, but had done around two hundred and fifty. Mike [2] said, 'I've done a thousand. That's more than all of you put together. How many gallbladders have you taken out?' They said, 'Well, we're obstetricians, we don't take organs out'. Mike [2] had taken out fifty. 'How many legs have you amputated?' 'We don't have to take legs off,' they said, 'these are pregnant women, we don't do stuff like that?'' He said, 'I've taken off twenty-five legs'. He literally went through his credentials. And he had more surgical experience than all of them put together in everything. Anyway, to cut a long story short, we got the paperwork sorted out and he got the job.

What have the two Mikes taught me? – You often reach difficult moments, difficult periods, and you just have to keep going for it. Never, ever be afraid to just make the difficult choices. And when you see an opportunity, you just go for it. No one wants to look back over the course of their life and have regrets; to have played small, and played safe. If an opportunity presents itself, just go for it. Because, at the very least, you're going to have a much more interesting life.

Go big or go home. It's much more interesting – you may have a disaster, but it's going to be interesting.

We need to learn to control our biology. When you panic it scrambles your biology, we say things we shouldn't say and act in a way we shouldn't. It's almost as if we lobotomize ourselves and the brain shuts down.

My team works with schools. We met a student called Dylan, the youngest of five; his dad's in prison and he's seen as massively disruptive in school. I sat him down with his teachers and explained that when people are under pressure, the brain shuts down. I asked Dylan to let me show him how it works. So, I put a clip on Dylan's earlobe and showed him a picture of his heart patterns. It was swinging widely up and down between 70 and 140 beats per minute in a chaos pattern. For us all, the fluctuations in heart rate become like an earthquake. It becomes very erratic, the signal from his heart shuts down the front part of our brains and means we don't think clearly. In this state, when we work on simple tasks, we fail.

And this is how we control it; breathe, a few rhythmic breaths. It's not deep breathing, it's rhythmic breathing. Rhythmic breath is a fixed ratio of the in breath to the out breath. Imagine you're breathing through the center of your chest, the heart area. So, the skill to stabilize your biology is to Breathe Rhythmically Evenly And Through the Heart, Every day – and guess what that spells: BREATHE.

Dylan learned something very important, he discovered there was something he could control. And it turns out, it was him.

Most human beings wander through life as victims. They are the victims of others. Your life will change literally forever if you take back ownership, stop blaming somebody else for how you feel. If people want to annoy me or upset me, or disappoint me, or frustrate me, they are going to need my permission. I decide whether I'm upset, or annoyed, or disappointed, or frustrated, not you.

The best people are always open for business. The best people are always on the hunt. They're always searching; the best people leave no stone unturned in the pursuit of excellence. They will talk to anybody, they'll be open, because you never know where killer insights are going to come from.

What about confidence and is it possible to have confidence regardless of external factors?

The sun shines, you shift from glum to cheerful. Why? Because the sun is shining. You have to train yourself to do so regardless of external forces. We can shift our emotions all the time on demand. In order to build confidence, remember any moment in your life, a moment when you did feel confident. For me, I wandered into this bar and sort of put my elbow on the counter. I was trying to attract attention. There was this beer mat right in front of me, I threw it across the bar literally about twenty-five feet away and it dropped into the bin, and everyone saw it. It was a fluke, but for a moment, I felt supremely confident. Just talking about it now, it's giving me a smile and I want to punch the air with confidence. When I feel less confident, I just reinstall that feeling myself to regain confidence, regardless of external forces.

What about fear? Fear might increase the energy levels and be a jump-start to action, but if you stay in fear it's a disabler, because the biology is in chaos and inhibits brain function. You have to move from fear to the positive side. Turn the fear into determination or excitement. We hear stage actors say, 'It's good that you're nervous before a performance,' but it's actually not true. They're confusing anxiety and fear with excitement, because the heart rates are about the same. But actually, if you're truly anxious, it's inhibits your performance. What you really want is determination and excitement.

I like to think that there is a 'universe of emotion' – in fact, there are thirty-four thousand emotions, like the number of planets in the universe. You all have a home planet. You wake up in the morning, on your home planet. For some it's called 'Not enough'; I didn't get enough sleep. I'm not getting enough money from Simon. I'm not getting enough clients. I'm not getting enough status. I'm not getting enough sex. I'm not getting enough... something.

My home planet is 'pathologically cheerful' – I've tried

being miserable, but what's the point? So, I wake up every day, unbelievably cheerful every morning.

To move between planets is difficult, as most people haven't got the navigational capability, because they're not paying attention to what's going on inside them. You need to start noticing, to start shifting to a planet that's more useful to you. It could be planet ruthless, or resolute, or confident, or excited, or exuberant, or determined, or focused. To stay on a planet, you've got to familiarize yourself with the experience – what does it really feel like to be on that planet? If you can describe it accurately to yourself, you can reinstall it at any point.

What is emotional health? People with anxiety or depression don't necessarily have anything wrong with their mental processes. All your cognitive processes are results driven by what you do. Your behavior is driven by what you think, your thinking is driven by what you feel, your feeling is driven by your emotions, and your emotions are driven by your biology. What we call mental health is really emotional development and emotional wellbeing.

What we need to do is learn to control our emotions. And if you can learn to control your emotions, it will be a game changer. An emotion is just the energy in motion of your body. It's all the biological energy that's constantly changing because we're constantly moving, our heart's constantly beating, and we're constantly digesting. There is a constant flux and there's energy in motion – that's your 'E motion'. A feeling is the awareness of that emotion. An emotion is the tune that the orchestra is playing, a feeling is the awareness of it."

– ALAN WATKINS

Reach Alan at *complete-coherence.com*

39

THIS WOMAN IS FABULOUS

JULY 30, 2020

A conversation with
HEATHER MONAHAN

HEATHER MONAHAN HAS dedicated her life to empowering others and pulling the curtain back to reveal what it takes to get ahead at work and in life, while leapfrogging the villains that you meet along the way. Heather has struggled with confidence her entire life. From the days living in a trailer with her mother and three siblings, to the day she was fired from her C-suite position by another woman, Heather has seen it all. Sat with a Britto painting in the background and her Apple earbuds in, she was a beacon of positivity for our talk. Heather tells her story of hard work and how it pays off.

"I have always looked for opportunities...

When working for a radio station, I saw that there was an opportunity to increase advertising revenue, so I pitched the CEO of the station a new role as CRO, which I would fill. When I went to close the CEO, he excused himself from the room for ten minutes. When he came back, he said, 'Okay, the role is yours'. I asked where he went and he said, 'I had to call my father to get his approval'.

Always pitch the decision-maker and never pitch someone who can say no but not say yes! Don't be fooled, if you are not getting the decision-maker, you are just running around in circles. (This line is my new favorite of all time!)

Then, after a time in the role as a Chief Revenue Officer, I was suddenly fired. I was shocked. That moment was devastating. I had no idea what the future held for me, and the feeling of uncertainty threatened to overwhelm me. I didn't know it at the time, but getting fired was the best thing that could have happened to me. I didn't realize that I had been dimming my light due to negative feedback. The CFO that I worked with was constantly upset with me. She would give me disapproving looks and belittle me, and instead of standing up for myself, I would shrink back in hope she would move on. I was wrong. The more I dimmed my light, the more she grew in power. As long as she remained in my life, I wasn't ever going to be confident. Being fired was where my journey to building confidence began.

I realized that, despite being fired, I kept all my experiences, talents, network, and unique value. While I didn't know it at the time, I was about to blow up the proverbial 'lanes' I had been limiting myself to. I would take my talents to become an author, a podcast host, keynote speaker, and executive coach. I realized I had been redirected, not rejected. The first thing I did when I got fired was ask for help, and the response was instant. All those people I had helped in the past reached out. Especially a friend who hosted a show on radio, when someone offers to help 'convert' that immediately as it happens – so I jumped at the chance of the radio interview.

I learned to jump into things, find out, watch, learn, and take the first steps. Fear now, for Heather, is a green light to go. I made mistakes along the way and then rebounded and just got on with things. For instance, I wanted to set up a line of clothing to complement my brand. It took nine months to prepare the line and I went to a major distributor with an amazing opportunity. They declined it. I had to embrace failure, evolve, and then pivot.

My mentor said to me one day, 'Pick your head up,' and I had no idea what he meant. So, I got on my peloton, this is my creative space to think – we all need space to think. I decided it was about not thinking small; focus on life as you want it to be and do something outside of your comfort zone. One of the many actions I took to live was to try stand-up comedy. What I discovered from doing this is that each of us have different fears, and confidence means different things for each of us. I realized that confidence was the key to my success.

How to build confidence is important. Once you have confidence, you can have anything you want. Until you have confidence, everything seems out of your reach. Confidence is all you need to have to dive in and get started. Confidence is like a muscle that needs to be developed daily, and can grow over time, and can be lost if you don't work at it.

The first step to confidence is to fire the villains in your life. We all have villains in our lives. Some of us work with our villains and some of us see them show up in our personal lives. It's up to each one of us to fire these villains or create boundaries to protect ourselves from them. In some cases, we can even be our own villains. When that's the case, we can rewrite the narrative we are telling ourselves. We can choose to show ourselves grace and speak to ourselves the same way we would a child or someone that we love dearly. No matter what form our villains take, firing them will set us up for our successful launch.

To change my villain narrative, I have a few techniques, set reminders - a soundtrack of my life – for instance, I have a rap playlist to listen to before every public speaking event. I have lavender scent with me and smell it, which takes me back to a time when I was crushing it! I visualize other talks, I gave my best, and to stop that internal villain, I practice and practice. When you decide to shine your light and be your authentic self, know that the haters will come. Sometimes, taking the risk to create and innovate will anger others.

And this led us to the concept of #bossinheels. For years I was told to dress in a certain way, act in a certain way, and not embrace who I am. This is the same for us all, male or female – we create fake versions of ourselves and will feel disempowered.

We need to show up as who we are, and then we feel good about ourselves. When we invest in ourselves, we can take a huge step forward. Show up as who you really are, creating all that you have within you. Now is your moment!

When we know who we are, then we value ourselves, and we can feel comfortable saying 'no' – remember, 'No' is a complete sentence, and you don't need to justify it or go beyond that. I remember a friend of mine, who was public speaking free of charge. I told her to 'be a true version of yourself and know your value, ask for payment, don't be afraid, know your worth.' When she started to do this, she got payment for all future talks she did."

– HEATHER MONAHAN

In her final thoughts Heather shared a couple of statements which she said have helped her:

Perfectly imperfect done is always better than perfect and doing nothing.

Lions do not lose sleep over the opinions of sheep, and neither will I.

If you want to connect with Heather, visit *heathermonahan.com*

40

MY COACHING PARTNER

SEPTEMBER 3, 2020

A conversation with
LUCAS JADIN

WHEN LUCAS TURNED UP in September 2020, I didn't know the journey we would go on together. He graciously offered to help, and after the talk we chatted about him coaching me one-to-one. There was something different about him, I really liked his style, and I am grateful to him for being by my side through this adventure, keeping me on point, and consistently challenging the best version of me to show up. I have multiple coaches and mentors, but what Lucas offered was something unique.

It was relatively early somewhere in Ohio when Lucas joined our Zoom; he was up to inspire. He is a co-author of Chop Wood Carry Water, a book which most of the office had read and a fable we loved. As a reminder he told the story of John the builder.

"John was recognized as the best builder in the county, with a thirty-year reputation as the person you should go to when you want to have a quality house built...

There came a time in John's life when he felt it was time to retire. So, he went to see his boss and explained how grateful he was to have worked with him for thirty years and been able to work at something he was passionate about. His boss was full of praise for John and asked him for a final favor. 'John,' he said, 'we have a very important client we have to build a house for, and I would appreciate it if you could work on it, as they are very dear to us, and this will be the last house you work on'. John said yes. The problem was John's heart was not in it. He felt that he was doing it out of an obligation to his boss, and as he built the house, he delegated work he hadn't previously done, he took a few shortcuts, and completed the house quicker than he usually took. The house was to a good standard, just not up to John's usual high standard.

Once the property was finished, a retirement party was thrown for John, and at the beginning of the evening his boss stood up and thanked John from all the company and those present in the room. He asked John to come on the stage and he handed him a small box. John opened the box and inside was a key; it was the key to the house John had just built. John's heart dropped; he thought to himself, if I had known the house was going to be mine, I would have taken more care.

How are you building your house today? How would you build it today, looking backwards? If only I had known, I would have done things differently. Like John, we spend time doing things for other people's 'houses' and we forget to build our own house. There are 86,400 seconds in a day – do you think of these seconds as a gift or a hindrance? How many of those seconds are you using to build your house effectively? Are you really taking care of you?

The sad truth is so many are looking to cut corners, everybody just wants to go back to normal. Me, I didn't want to go back, I wanted to go forward to a newer, more exciting future.

This story was super powerful in the current moment; everyone is looking for shortcuts, not many have patience and a desire to do a great job, so this story was really important.

(H)E+R=O

Whatever the event, plus the way you respond to it, equals the outcome. We use the same equation at Ink, and during the last couple of years we added the H to create HERO. There's a story of a fighter pilot instructor, who, when training future fighter pilots, put them through a series of tests to assess how they would perform and respond under pressure. His name for this was OBE – will they be overcome by events. So, what he would do is crank up the events they had to face in a simulator to see how much they could take before they cracked or broke down.

How much pressure can we take, and how do we raise our own ability to be overcome by events? Do we react with anxiety, anger, isolation, doubt, inadequacy, and fear? If we do, then we need to be aware of this. This awareness will help us deal with an OBE situation. In those situations, we need to release energy, we need to have belief and passion. I have three fundamental areas I focus on to do this – eating healthy, making connections, and working out. The solution for me was simple, yet it wasn't easy. I track daily what I do, and that helps me cope in those extreme OBE situations.

Another way is that I filter the messages I get, externally and internally. Filtering the messages' meanings from fear, insecurity, and self-doubt, as this creates confirmation bias, and when I hear those messages, everything that then happens supports my meanings. We need to slow down, be aware, and decide to sink below those feelings; you need to understand that those messages come from your reptilian brain. It's a built-in process wanting to protect us. I call it the 'little voice', the voice which causes us to be fearful and consider the worst-case scenario. We need to ask ourselves, is that voice true in the current situation? Don't fight it, just give it space to do its thing, to do its job. We then need to decide if we want to listen to it or not.

Life doesn't happen with certainty, yet we want certainty, and this causes friction. The way to handle this friction is to remember that each day you are building your own house and are evolving. The other thing is that this friction can cause our 'twin thieves' to shout out loud. These thieves rob us of our joy, success, and create limiting beliefs.

We need to understand that the best moments in life are preceded by nervousness and when we think we are broken. This is important to know and be aware of, as it gives those nerves a different meaning – nerves are about growth.

In medieval times, a sword-smith was known as a Toko. Their job was to take metal, heat it up in fire at an incredible temperature, melt it, then pound it into shape, and repeat over and over again. They did this till the sword was strong, light, and sharp. Only by following this process were the best swords produced. In your life, when have you been through the fire? Remember those times. Those times were hard, yet you learned to do those hard things. We all have been forged through experiences and come out stronger. Take at least three minutes each day to remember those times and tap into that emotion. When we remember those times, we know if we face them again we will be better equipped to deal with them."

- LUCAS JADIN

Lucas' story made me realize that many of my leaders were really struggling and starting to be overcome by the current events. We decided at this point to sit down and see what we could do to help them. We went off site and brainstormed and challenged each other how we can bring the magic back, without a clear end in sight. The leak in the boat was getting bigger and the faith amongst my team was waining.

Don't look for validation externally, it comes from within. We may have all the financial success, yet if internally we still live in a state of feeling unsatisfied and remain anxious, fearful, and in doubt, then the external validation will be pointless. Mastery is achievement, and not based on success. It's based on what you learned and can learn, it's about growth and the achievement of being a free individual and being unlocked from inhibitors.

I really liked his traffic light analogy. Picture traffic lights – Lucas sees his day in terms of traffic lights:

- Green – is when I see flow, and release my full energy.
- Yellow/amber – I see a water pipe with a kink in it. The water is flowing through the kink, yet the flow is hindered.
- Red – is about trapped energy. The water in

the pipe is bottled up and ready to explode, and not in a good way.

It's funny, one of my favorite reads during this period was *Greenlights* by Matthew McConaughey, and my interpretation was that a red light was not to stop; it was to pause, look around, get ready, be prepared, and take a breather before you continue on your journey. Green was not just about go, go, go, it was to make sure you are going in the right direction, make sure you have all you need to make the journey successful. These are two different viewpoints, and I loved them both.

In his final story, Lucas tells us about the founder of Judo, Kano Jigoro Shihan.

On his deathbed, he was asked by his students what they could do to help him prepare for the afterlife and the next world transition. The master said, "bury me with a white belt, as wherever I am going, I want to be there as a beginner." He wanted a white belt mentality whilst developing a black belt mindset. Despite all he had achieved, he approached death as he approached life; like a beginner.

Thinking like a beginner creates a learning velocity and a mastery mindset – one of adapting and growing. Lucas asked my team, "Are you willing to wear a white belt?" I guess this and Chris's talk inspired me to write *White Belt Thinking*.

Lucas can be reached at *t2bc.com*

41

THE DREAM ARCHITECT

OCTOBER 15, 2020

A conversation with
TRAVIS FOX

DURING THE PANDEMIC, Brad Lea asked me to come and do a talk for his Closer School Academy. After the talk, this charming man followed me and was incredibly kind. I listened to what he had to say and thought my team would love this message, so in October Travis joined us for a wonderful enlightening session.

For a quarter of a century, Travis Fox has been known as 'The Dream Architect', helping individuals map out step-by-step blueprints for lives they really want to live.

"Family, when you're looking for someone who can completely transform your life for the better or someone to get business advice from, then listen to this...

Who is the person you have the longest relationship with? And yes, 'family', it's with yourself. So why do we spend time talking to ourselves so badly? Would you have friends if you talked to them the way you talk to yourself?

Did you know that buyers decide in six seconds if they are going to buy from you, so what this tells us is that we need to connect on an emotional and relationship level. Be aware that conversations don't just happen at a conscious level, it goes deeper. There are three levels we need to be aware of:

Conscious – awareness, subconscious – belief, and super or shadow conscious - emotions. Most salespeople connect via the conscious level with logic, and what they should connect at is the super or shadow conscious level. One tip Travis gave us was to tell stories, as these are provocative, attach to the emotions, and as a conclusion, have a form of call to action.

It's all about a transfer of enthusiasm; it's our responsibility to convey enthusiasm and connect. When we transfer this enthusiasm, we need to understand the cognitive process. Did you know that 95% of all our actions are automatic? We are in reaction mode. Our mind has been hypnotized and is in script mode. This condition is there as a defensive posture to keep us safe.

As an example, if we say 'how are you?', we – especially men – don't really want to have an answer. This is a process, it's not being in a feeling state, which is why most people answer 'fine' – as a funny aside, 'fine' means fucked up, insecure, neurotic, and emotional. People when asked the question need to assign a meaning to respond. So, ask a different question like What's the most interesting thing that has happened to you today? Are you right- or left-handed? This gets the buyer out of reaction mode. It will also move us from 'no' to knowing.

How long does a game of golf last? In my case, fourteen hours! The answer is actually forty-two minutes; the rest of the time is getting a tan between shots. It's between the shots that is important. It's during that time we internally review and give negative feedback to ourselves about the game, and this will impact on our performance.

It's the same on a sales call. It's the space between calls that is the most important; what we say to ourselves between calls. The dialogue will set the emotion for the next call. Are we talking like a positive friend, and if not, what you need to do is reset the emotion positively? Otherwise, we will transfer negative emotion to the person we are interacting with and not a transfer of enthusiasm. It's an emotional rollercoaster –

or the 'Kick the Cat' syndrome. Imagine Dad has a bad sales day, comes home and yells at Mum, then Mum yells at the kids because Dad has had a bad day. Kids go to their room asking 'What did we do?' and kick the cat, and the cat – to prove it's in control – coughs off a fur ball and is sick on the floor!

TRANSFER ENTHUSIASM AND NOT THE NEGATIVITY.

I had been playing golf since I was five, largely encouraged by my dad. Early on in my career, I suffered a severe eye injury which almost left me completely blind in my left eye. By my senior year of high school, I was on track to be a professional golfer. I thought it was my true passion and destiny. And then my high school sweetheart became pregnant, and she did the unthinkable – the child was given up for adoption without my agreement or knowledge. To say this destroyed me doesn't give the feeling I had justice; I was in pieces, my golf game suffered, and I questioned what life was all about. I realized that if something is not truly your passion, then you should not feel forced to do it.

Who we think we are, the baseplate of thought all your thinking and actions come from, are influenced and programmed by what are known as four pillars, and they are mother, father, religion, and state. These drive emotional compulsion, which drives our belief system. Often, we have to step away from those influences and realize the noble truth. What's the noble truth? We are not getting off this planet alive! Let me ask you: if you had thirty days to live, would you be acting and thinking like you are right now? If not, change it. When you clip into something bigger than yourself, your passion shows up. You understand your purpose, you have a blueprint, and you know what to do every day.

Being aware of what defines our thoughts, actions, and how we talk to ourselves is partway to transferring positive energy into our lives. We have to change the automatic processes and conversations we have with ourselves, as well as those with our customers."

- TRAVIS FOX

You can reach out to Travis by searching Travis Fox on LinkedIn.

42

OCTOBER 2020

I WAS EXHAUSTED. Maybe I had learned too much, had too many thoughts going through my head. I had really learned a lot about myself during these six months. I really was thinking about stuff in a different way.

I decided to book no more speakers. In some ways, inspiring people, making them feel limitless and motivated, was actually helping them on their way. The market was still soft, Asia still very much locked down, Europe dribbling back, we were finding it hard to sell much. In the US, travel was starting to improve, traffic at 30–40% of what it was in 2019. We were selling bits and pieces, but nobody really cared about travelers. Rioting in Philly, stabbings in Nice; the world was a mess. Trump got Covid, the election was heating up. I was in Miami and recorded a video, I am fucking fed up of the word 'no'. 'Yes' is the destination, 'no' is how you get there. Too many people cannot see the wood for the trees. It's not easy, but getting out of this mess was never going to be easy.

I reached out to Gary Vaynerchuk, aka Gary Vee,

and asked him to guest edit *American Way*. He and his team agreed. Got to get this show back on the road. Sadly, the magazine stopped before we got a chance to make it happen. It's another reminder that what you think is good today, doesn't always turn out to be good in the end. Only in time will you be able to look back and decide if it was a good thing or not. That event might not have turned out the way I wanted, but the confidence to pick up the phone and ask was definitely a positive moment. I kept asking myself all the way through this period, is my thinking making this situation better or worse?

Remember your life will only have some meaning, if you give meaning to your life.

43

NOVEMBER 2020

LEARNING SO MUCH from all these guys was so powerful, and you don't need a crisis to take on board some of the thinking in these chapters. One thing I did notice was people starting to lose faith in the business. When you coach anybody, they get better, believe in themselves to be the best version of themselves, and slowly, one by one, the members of my team started to leave the business. The calls became more frequent – "It's not you, it's me. I am so grateful for what you did for me."

My best sellers, my leaders, people who had been with me for nearly a decade started to flee the nest. I could not do anything to stop them, I didn't have a way for them to make the same money anymore. It remains one of the saddest periods of my commercial career. I lost over a hundred quality people, and only one decided to be difficult – such a shame he went the way he did. I believe in karma. I believe that one day, he will realize he was wrong. When he reads this, maybe. He blamed everybody, he was bitter and angry, despite us looking after him for many years. We should have sacked him a year earlier, yet due to our good nature, we made every effort to keep employed, especially as he came here after his own business went bankrupt. We were bloody good to him; he had free counseling to manage his out-of-work challenges and we sent him all over the world, but in response he attacked us when we were on our knees. I forgive, but I will never forget. I don't mind accepting criticism when we make mistakes, when we are to blame, but we didn't create this pandemic, we didn't stop the airlines taking off, and we all lost lots. I am and will always be grateful to those who stood by us, who believed in us, who believed that travel would return, and who I am doing my best to reward for their loyalty and support.

With hindsight, this was a gift; it was a magical time, a time when we all learned a lot about ourselves. A time when we grew as a team, learned gratitude, and allowed ourselves to be better humans. We did lots of charity work, raised money, got fit, learned new things, and made amazing montages, videos and lists to change our and others' worlds. It was a time when we forgot about greed and replaced it with appreciation and we were full of new ideas of who we wanted to come out of this period as. Better humans, kinder people, with wider periphery of life. We took a long, hard look in the mirror. I realized that with one candle, I could light hundreds of candles, and that's what I did. I learned that we cannot save everybody, but the ones that I did, turned out to be better teammates, and the results showed.

44

DECEMBER 2020

IN THE WORDS OF MOTHER THERESA, I know God will not give me anything I can't handle. I just wish that he didn't trust me so much. After all the shit 2020 had thrown at us, as we entered December it was important to look back at the year. The US had a new president, Brexit was starting to play havoc with Europe, there were so many highs and lows, social and racial injustice, rioting, looting, marching, and protests continued throughout the year.

It was a hard year. Five hundred thousand people died from Covid and we lost Kobe Bryant in a helicopter crash. Farmers say that every seven years you need to let the land just rest for a year. Maybe that's what 2020 was all about. We had time, and we didn't enjoy it – it's hard to relax while your business is falling around you. It's hard to appreciate what you have when you could lose it at any moment.

It's also difficult to look for positives in so much negativity. Yet, in my usual lucky style, I managed to make the best out of it that I could. The family had a holiday or two, we had multiple stay-cations, and we walked and talked a lot. I got to spend quality time with the ones I loved, and I got what I had always been craving for: more time to think. With the benefit of hindsight, securing all these amazing speakers, and them and us having the time to spend together would never have happened otherwise, and I would not have learned so much.

In my house, my youngest son was turning thirteen, my middle son had a professional football contract, and Lady Lucky Leslie, my third horse, was about to race for the first time. The first two didn't make it – I learned why racing is such an expensive sport. I co-owned my first horse with one of the greatest horse trainers on the planet; I assumed he knew a thing or two about racing, I was wrong. The second horse was a beast, loved the female horses, and had a bad temper. They say animals are like their owners. He kicked the stable one night and sadly had to be put down.

So here we are on December 19th, and a new strain of the virus emerges, European countries start to ban the UK citizens from entering, Christmas is canceled, we are back in lockdown, my footballer son breaks his leg, my other son's bar mitzvah is canceled, and on my horse's first ride, she leads the field in to the home straight, she looks graceful until the final two furlongs. She disappears from the tv screen, I remember thinking I must have missed her. Sadly not, she has had a breakdown and collapsed and after a few frantic phone calls with the trainer is put to sleep.

It is really important to understand that nothing is permanent, every single thing can come and go, and if we can live with that understanding, we can avoid so many upsets. It is not easy, but with enough practice, we can achieve better ability in all parts of our life. I think I learned much of this skill during the year. If I had allowed things to get me down every time the wind changed, I would have struggled with serious emotional wellbeing issues. Instead, I feel calm, balanced, and at peace with life. I am grateful for so much and comfortable with everything that has happened, good or bad.

We will never know if it is good or really bad until we look back in years to come. Right now, they were just events, and I did my best to be present with all of them, positive or negative. I can tell you that, as a business, in June, we estimated we would lose five million dollars. As the year ended, we lost over ten million dollars, when a year earlier we had made just shy of fourteen million dollars – that's what you call - a mess.

Vaccines are coming, this will all be over soon. I take two of the boys to Antigua and we have Christmas and New Year in style. Sadly, my wife and son stay in London for his foot operation. The kids headed home and I went off to the US. Let's see what we can do in Miami for a few weeks. A few weeks turn into months. I am away from home for twelve weeks in total, in which time I attempt to salvage the business. It's important to recognize that without the constant commitment of my wife, my boys and my friends, I would have been broken. I put on a brave face, I was miserable and at times felt incredibly alone.

45

JANUARY 2021

BACK IN MARCH 2020, we thought this would be over in a few weeks, the most pessimistic said September. Here we are in January 2021, starting a new year in lockdown. Arriving in Miami, I saw the traffic from the plane, it looked normal, and it was. Despite a high number of cases, Miami was operating as always; restaurants were full, not many were wearing masks, and business continued as normal. I spent the first quarter away from home, trying hard to salvage what was left on the Titanic. I will explain the irony of this statement later.

Asia was on high alert, everything closed down, Europe was on lockdown, and here I was playing tennis and cycling to the beach. Sometimes being in the right place at the right time is what makes things happen. My colleague arrived from London, and could not understand what was going on; here we were, sitting in a packed restaurant, drinking ice cold Coronas. Washington was under siege and things just seemed to carry on.

A super analogy is that it was like everyone was given a fresh big box of Lego, and right now we all had an opportunity to build something new. Some built cars, planes, and trains. Some just started and never finished. Some didn't even start. I decided I would build a new business.

In order to give myself a way to de-stress, I started writing poems, and published them on Instagram under the name of @themotivationalpoet. Four line poems, shared how I was feeling and the emotions I was going through. Any catchy phrases that I saw or heard would become a poem. It gave me an outlet to be curious, creative and calm. When people all round the world started to share them, I thought, I might be on to something here.

JANUARY 12TH

CNN announced that they would close their Airport TV network. Having invested in Reach TV in 2019, this was music to my ears. They had lost confidence in the arena. I didn't want any of our competitors to buy it, and if we secured it, it would be game changing for our business. Total dominance of the airport TV space.

It was a huge opportunity, and we were presented with a wall of disinterest. CNN had made a decision and it was final. I am sure it would cost them tens of millions of dollars to shut down this network. We held multiple conference calls and despite 'No' after 'No', I refused to back down. Normally, I go to seven 'No's. I was in double digits. We went military style, attacking all the airports, doing our best to convince them to move over to our network.

Approaching the end of January, we got one last chance when one airport suggested that we propose to take over their contracts. That's all I needed; in the next call, I was up to twelve 'No's when one of my suggestions seemed to strike a chord. And instead of 'No', it was 'let me take that back to the team'. Had I got my foot in the door? I was proposing to save jobs, save millions of dollars, and help the airports not to lose a great communication with their passengers. It was a win-win for everyone. This could be game-changing for our business, and here I was fighting the fight. The network was shutting off on March 31st; we had two months to pull off the greatest deal of our lives. Lynnwood (AKA Woody), who founded the network, and I started to plan our attack to win over as many airports as we could. We set up our war room and went from airport to airport telling them our story. It was compelling and many loved our vision and spirit. Yet these were governmental organizations and there was going to be many hoops and paperwork to jump through.

46

FEBRUARY 2021

THE FIRST OF THE MONTH and we got a green light to talk to the airports; it was full steam ahead... We were competing with some of the biggest names in outdoor media. One day they wanted to be our friends, the next day they were stabbing us in the back. Don't trust anyone, I kept thinking to myself and telling Woody. Until we got signatures on paper, we had nothing. We needed to secure New York's four airports – that was the key to this deal.

"When we pull this off, it's a story we will be able to tell our grandkids," I remember telling Woody. Here we were, a depleted business, dying on its feet, and at the same time securing one of the finest inventories in the US outdoor market. We had to secure funding, letters of credit, and prove to the airports we were good for the fees. And to convince our own investors that we could do this.

It was a funny call. "Why the hell do you think you can sell this, when the mighty CNN have failed," our lead investor asked? I said, "That's why you don't pay me enough." After he cleaned up his spat-out soda, he asked again. "We are selling now, when all around us in this space have given up. We are not giving up and this is prime media, we will succeed at this." At the same time, our investors were closing a reverse buyout and were unable to help with funding, but no way was I going to lose this deal. I remember saying this was a huge problem and they needed to find a way. Over the next eight weeks, we secured forty letters of credit in a timeframe I have never seen and, one by one, signed the airports up. We did it, we grew our existing network and went from the number two player to the only proper airport TV network. Common sense, even though it seemed not that common, prevailed.

Now we had to sell the adverts, fix the technology, and build a bigger business. As one door opened, another heap of shit was coming our way. Our biggest client, who had kept publishing throughout the pandemic, decided to terminate our contract. To make things worse, my friend, my colleague, and sales mastermind behind many of our success stories – his nine-year-old daughter was diagnosed with cancer. I needed to help him, cover him, and support him in the best way I could. He needed to be home and I looked after his job for him. In the same week, my mother was diagnosed with dementia, don't worry, I remember saying to myself, I can deal with all of this. Again this is me at my best, more balls to juggle,

I can manage it. It's a horrible time, seeing children and parents suffering. Oh, and Harry and Megan are being shits to the British monarchy, I feel sorry for the Queen.

Is this enough stress for one human to deal with? I am missing home terribly. It was at this moment I remember thinking, how you do anything is how you do everything.

47

MARCH 2021

ADRENALINE WAS KEEPING me going as I was fighting fires, dealing with more people leaving, working out how to deal with the loss of the only inflight magazine in the US sky, and getting ready to close the CNN deal by the deadline. Stupidly, among our senior team, there are bruised egos everywhere, but I'm doing my best to hold it all together. My blood pressure is on the rise, the stress is enormous, and I have been away from home for twelve weeks. I am living out of a suitcase, eating badly, and living on days of high and low energy.

On 31st March we switched over dozens of airports and we are live; now we have to sell some adverts to pay for this. CNN left the cupboard bare, so we had to build from nothing. Travel was starting to return, but advertisers were not coming back very quickly. Our cash was running out and we had to go cap in hand to get some more. It was not something I wanted to do.

Our board meeting was insane. The board were asking stupid questions, apparently, we were the only company in the group who were a basket-case, everyone else was back in business. Harry and Megan do an Oprah interview, some feel sorry, some continue to think they are not very nice people.

We conduct staff surveys with the few people who are left; as you can imagine, the morale is low, the anxiety is high, and I am not giving anyone a cause to believe in, let alone me. The accountants are forecasting we will do fifty-five million dollars this year, and I laugh out loud. I reiterate we will do whatever we can, I can't budget realistically now, it's pure guesswork. The only thing I can predict is more crap is on its way.

We are 52 weeks in and I am not sure how much more of this I can personally take.

What I start to realize as I type this book, is that I am not in a good place, and I wonder how many books are written by people in a bad place, telling people how to get to a better place. It's what I need to do, to change my own state. This is certainly helping me get the mind and body fit for purpose.

48

APRIL 2021

HERE WE WERE, the first month of us selling the bigger network, me and four guys in London. Yes, you read that right, we were selling a US television network from London.

In the four weeks post-deal, we amassed more revenue than had been done in the previous two quarters. My premonition was correct. We had secured a great asset and we were on the road to recovery. Within days of going live, we had enquiries about selling the business. No way, this was a golden asset. Flights started opening up again, and then in a flash they stopped. We got this stupid red, green and amber watchlist, and they kept changing, so no one knew if they should book or not. The uncertainty was killing my team's morale, and ability to deliver.

I regularly kept in touch with Mark Goulston, Lucas and Sanyika, others would check in from time to time. I built a new circle of influence and it felt helpful for me to have this group as the new Ink was forming.

49

MAY/JUNE 2021

WHAT HAPPENED NEXT was quite scary. I had had enough. I had arrived at a place where relief and stress clashed. I am unsure how I felt, elated or exhausted. I was falling apart; the turmoil of the last fourteen month was suddenly hitting me. I had stopped the leaks, I had rearranged the deckchairs, and having spent the last year looking after everyone else, making sure everyone else came first, here I was, depleted and broken. Nothing left in the tank, fed up with snide comments from employees, colleagues, investors. I was constantly feeling like the pantomime villain.

We had turned around a business, which had lost all its clients, and bought a digital business, which was counter to what everyone in the space was doing, because we believed in the founders' vision. We negotiated amazing deals for the company and saved a business that had died and took huge pay cuts to keep everyone whole, and now here I was asking for a bit more money to look after the leadership team. I was flatly refused. This sent me into a spiral of depression.

Did they not understand how much I had sacrificed to save this business, being away from home for months on end, long hours, to save a business that should not still be here?

I couldn't even begin to measure how much personal sacrifice, in my own health, marriage, and family I had endured. My commitment to the cause just seemed to be swept under the carpet and the gratitude and appreciation I craved were nowhere to be seen. I thought it was funny; all the way through I had remained positive and banished negative thoughts, and here I was, nearly through the mess, and all I could see was negativity.

It was very clear that, rather than being seen as an asset to the business, I was being treated like a liability. Even in these conversations, I was being made to feel like 'Oliver'.

I remember typing these words: "I am not going to leave anyone high and dry, but for my own sanity I think I need to find an amicable exit from the business." After twenty-six years, my journey felt like it was coming to an end. I got up at 4:45am and sent a long email to all my partners and investors, spelling out how I felt. Some were sympathetic, others saw me as a problem, and frankly, if I didn't want to do the job, they would find someone else. Good luck, I remember thinking.

I wasn't feeling well, my son at twenty-two had just been diagnosed with diabetes which upset me a lot. It was Friday morning and I went to see a doctor. My blood pressure was 162/122, and he told me to take a month off work. I flatly ignored him and went straight to the office. I helped close a few big deals, and dealt with our latest Covid outbreak in our Miami office before heading home at 7pm. On that journey home, I decided I had to take a break. The next week I went to my seaside home and relaxed, worked on myself, ate healthily, juiced, and read. By the end of the week, I was out of scary territory, and by week three I was back down to normal blood pressure. My team was superb and rallied around and took the slack; we nearly broke even for the month. Even typing that felt good.

50

JULY 2021

I WAS REALLY FED UP with all the negativity surrounding me. It was my birthday month and I was going to treat myself to some retail therapy. I booked a trip to Saint Lucia with the family, so I could get back to the States. Two weeks out of Europe would get me in, and I would bring the family with me for the summer holidays.

The noise in England was that the national football team might win the Euro Football tournament, as they had reached their first final in sixty years. My kids wanted to go, tickets were trading at four thousand pounds each. I was all over my connections, trying to get tickets and was on the verge of giving up. I say on the verge, cos I never want to give up, I keep making more and more enquiries. In the background I decided, you know what, I have never been to a men's final at Wimbledon, so I secured a hospitality ticket for me and the wife to watch that instead, as it was the same date as the Euros final anyhow. I was excited to be seeing Novac live. On the Friday night before, an ex-employee reached out from France; would I like four tickets to the final? The price was much less than the market rate, but still a lot of money. My boys would be ecstatic.

This is what savings were for – oh, I didn't have any savings left! I thought fuck it, it might never happen again in my or their lifetime, let's do it. We agree on the cost and I try to PayPal the money. It fails. No way, so close. What happened next was an act of genuine kindness and trust. She sent me the tickets and said to transfer the money next week. This was over ten thousand pounds. Really!

It's another reminder that if you are kind, people will be kind in return. She said, "Just send me a pic with your boys." Was this happening, was I going to win Dad of the year award? Yep, it really happened, and I got to see the men's final, sitting next to Royals and Tom Cruise, enjoying cream tea. It was frightfully civilized. I drove as fast as I could from Wimbledon to Wembley – as did TC and the Royal family - to see England lose on penalties to Italy. What an amazing day; the pictures of me and my boys at this final will remain etched in my memory, along with a wonderful day of tennis.

Like every high in the past year, the low followed quite quickly. Within days, I had Covid. I picked it up at the final, along with many others. Two weeks of hell followed, as I was barely able to stay awake for longer than a few hours. I slept and slept. I think the last fifteen months of adrenaline was being released from my body. Every argument, every challenge, every up and down was coming out in aches and pains. Our trip to Saint Lucia and the States was kiboshed. Everyone was gutted.

Sometimes in life you need to draw a line in the sand. I think this month was my line; it was the start of my mental rebound. Having time to rethink, I was starting to see the world through rosier tinted glasses. I wasn't there yet, but definitely felt the tide was turning and the momentum was going in the right direction. This was the moment I started to believe again. I need to give everyone a cause to believe in and a leader to trust. How could everyone else be positive, if I was in such negative territory?

51

AUGUST 2021

WITH COVID GONE, the next thing to go was my foot – a rather aggressive game of tennis had left me so injured I could not walk. An MRI showed I had torn through my foot, so I had to spend sixteen weeks in a boot. As I sat in the hospital, I wrote to the hotels in Saint Lucia and Miami and got the trips back on track – in two weeks, I would be free of Covid for a month and able to travel again.

The preparations started and we had the most wonderful time as a family; we ate, drank, and played cricket on the beach, even in my boot. My family went home and one of my sons came to Miami with me. We would spend the next three weeks doing deals, negotiating transactions, and generally feeling positive. Then an opportunity presented itself that was too good to miss. As a boy, I had always wanted to ring the bell at the stock exchange, and my parent company was doing so this next week. I checked flights; I could be there. Yes, I would go.

The whole experience was awesome, just being at the Nasdaq, standing where many great CEOs had stood before me, was surreal. Seeing myself on CNBC and Bloomberg was a great moment for my parents, although my dad asked "Why are you dressed so scruffily?"

All our faces were splashed over Times Square, it was a magical moment and one I am grateful to Stagwell for allowing me to be part of. Dreams do come true.

I realized that the US open was on, so I suggested to my son, let's go to the final. Having been to the men's final at Wimbledon, I settled for the women's final, and boy am I a lucky human. The British player, nineteen-year-old Emma Raducanu had made it through from qualifying to the final. Was I going to witness the first British winner for 50 years? It was an amazing final, and she did it, we saw it, with the travel ban, there were very few supporting Emma, we made ourselves heard as she lifted the trophy. Life is always about being in the right place at the right time. I love serendipity.

Then more magic happened, Woody agreed a deal with the NFL for our Reach television network to show live football games at the airport. Yes, we were going to be selling the Super Bowl. The greatest sporting occasion on the sports calendar along with five games every weekend. We were the only network to have every game. At the time it was a big commitment, we had to do it and thankfully everyone was supportive of us. We were about to enter the big league. The home of live sports in travel would be our new tagline. A year earlier we were on the verge of going out of business. Yet here we are doing mega deals with the world greatest partners. I always believe someone is looking down on me, and I continue to give back as much as I can to say thank you in my own little way.

The momentum has changed in our favor, and I believe, with a capital B.

52

SEPTEMBER 2021

I HAD RUNG THE BELL at the Nasdaq. I was feeling energized and excited as I flew back to Miami to get the team ready for Q4.

As I sat in Miami, no one knew how fed up I was. I had spent the first week inspiring the team, attempting to give them a cause to continue believing in. Despite the performance, morale and belief was really low. They were living in the past, and I was doing my best to encourage them to believe that the future would be even more exciting.

The following day was to be a big one, the first live one-to-one with my bosses in two years. Was this going to be my last day, or would I continue to steer the ship? Six months earlier, I had asked for the senior team to be remunerated; many of us had not had a raise or any bonuses in years. It was flatly rejected. I was told that the captain of the Titanic didn't get any more money for trying to save his boat, and that we were the worst company in the group. I wiped my mouth and carried on. To be fair, this was after I had a tantrum and threw all my toys out of the pram! Now I was happy to accept whatever outcome we would agree to. I would be happy to stay, happy to leave or even somewhere in the middle.

Was tomorrow going to be a moment I would look back on? What is funny, and its only my opinion, is that my bosses actually like and value me, they just have no patience for me, and find my style aggressive and demanding. I always say, who do you want working for you, a shit negotiator or an assassin? Yes, I was a pain in the arse, but by heck did I deliver. Over the last year, Chris Voss, Dr. Goulston, and Sanyika had helped me with various negotiations. They had become friends and mentors during this process. They kept me sane while I was struggling with people who didn't see my vision, didn't believe my predictions. My predictions, in the end, were Nostradamus-like. We smashed the numbers out of the park. We eeked back into profit.

The sun was shining in Washington, we had tapas in the street, and I felt like I had been transported to Barcelona. The weather was so much nicer than it was in Miami. At the meeting, there was lots of finger-pointing and accusations; it was a great game of tug of war. We spent the next couple of hours in the boardroom, debating the merits of my requests, with me trying to understand the commercial logic behind the refusal. By the end of it, I was still employed, my team would be happy with me. We had to get the business back into significant profit by the end of the year. As we finished September, another small profit had reduced our losses to circa one million dollars for the year, having peaked nearer seven million a few months earlier. I had to close out the year in profit, I had to deliver so that everybody got paid. I have no issues with pressure when the motivation is in place. My team felt the same way, and they were excited by the challenge.

My focus was on winning big deals and finding more great acquisitions for the company. Bring it on baby, that's what I love doing, doing deals and helping fix people's problems. Two days later I was standing around our boardroom table with a company which I think we can take globally. Let's see if I can make this happen.

PlayersTV is a network with content from professional sports players, owned and run by them also. They had great content and great ideas, they just needed a commercial team to help. They needed TV distribution, which we had, and a studio to make stuff TICK. This was in our sweet spot. Let's get a deal done. The negotiations began.

As I left Miami, it had been a hugely productive three weeks, and the team were focused. I had promised them the holiday party of all parties, and boy did I mean it. We were going to pull out all the stops, bring people from Singapore and London too. We were going to celebrate a year we not only survived, but thrived, too. Everybody was focused, all had super targets, all wanted to do things again. We were doing incentives. We were flying people around the world to do business again. It was starting to feel real. Yet the new team in London had no reference point for what 'good' looked like. In an office that used to hold eighty-ish sales people, today only twenty came to work some days of the week. A sneeze, a cough kept people off for days on end; it was a nightmare trying to get momentum. We were in the rebuilding phase and this was going to be a mission to get our special Ink energy back.

53

OCTOBER 2021

OCTOBER HAD EVEN MORE challenges, this time our printers could not deliver on time. We can't just be late, we can't come out three weeks late. My team conceded defeat, I don't do defeat. So, I went about finding someone who could help me, and I was as lucky as ever. I found out that the person dealing with us had been out to dinner with me ten years earlier. You never know when the kindness you deliver will be paid back, and late on that Friday night in October, mine was returned. The chap had pulled some favors and got our printing back on track. That conversation stopped a two-million-dollar black hole. Big calls, big challenges are what I live for. I was probably a firefighter in a previous life.

The Players team came to London and we agreed a deal. Nothing like a good night out in London to secure your deal. An NFL game at the Tottenham Hotspur stadium sealed it, and we would launch a European version in 2023. It was a great deal for both parties and I was super pumped to make it happen.

I was on the road again, this time traveling to Budapest to give a talk to Corvinus University business students on sales. It was lovely to stay in a nice hotel again – it had been a while, as the place in Miami was not that nice. The feedback was wonderful. I love working with young people, helping them find their path in life.

Positive news started to come through; the US said we could enter in November, Singapore opened up a few travel lanes, and traffic numbers started to improve. The number of people dying was on the increase in the UK, none of this made any sense. To add to the non-sense, I decide its abundance only from here onwards; I am living and enjoying my best life (I made a bit of money off crypto and shares too) and went out and bought myself a Bentley. I was back. I wanted to feel alive and was ready to enjoy every part of my life.

By the end of the month, we had delivered another profitable month and we were at break even for the year. It was looking good for the final push in Q4. Our board meeting was a fun affair; we were back, and everyone seemed excited for us.

We finished October with all our November products in record territory, and it wasn't not even the 1st of the month. I love it when momentum catches hold of you. So many campaigns were getting shunted into Q1, supply chain problems and chip shortages. Apple and Amazon reported poor results. We would find other money, we always do. My team would turn over every stone until we hit our targets; even with a depleted team, we are solid and the sales teams started to believe once again.

54

NOVEMBER 2021

HERE I AM in November 2021, the USA is open and the next thirty days presented opportunities and problems in equal measures. One thing I realized over the previous eighteen months is that complaining about the situation is nothing more than a waste of time. It won't change it and will leave you feeling crap. For the situation to get better, you need to get and think better.

My son had just turned twenty and we had Chinese food to celebrate. It was a lovely moment, with all the family together. The light at the end of the tunnel was coming back on. In October we pulled out another profitable month, and here I was starting to feel alive again. My home was full of sick people, it's hard to believe we had flu before Covid, as they seemed to be testing themselves daily. "You got the good old-fashioned flu," I said. After a couple of Covid tests I was ready to fly. Miami, here I come. What's funny is I had no idea of the four weeks that lay ahead of me. I made a decision; to stop giving away my time for free. I spent too many hours coaching colleagues; now if they wanted my time they needed to earn it. I was not going to do one-on-one coaching and watch them ignore my advice, I'd had enough of setting myself on fire to keep everyone else warm.

After a couple of days in the office, I decided to take up an invitation to go to a dude ranch. Weeks earlier, I had declined the opportunity and there I was at the 11th hour looking at flights. The office was in good shape and the numbers were also good, so a week out of the office would not harm the situation, and actually, with hindsight, turned out to be good for all of us. I hired a new sales training program for the company in the summer and decided to see if the owner was in Scottsdale. It turned out well; he was doing an offsite with twenty salespeople and invited me to come and speak. After my talk, they decided to take me out for dinner, it was the first big drinking evening for a while. A reallly good night out! The next day I hooked up with another couple of dudes in Scottsdale and we headed for the ranch – horse riding, archery and shooting was the order of the week. It was a great time spent with eighty blokes, many of them highly successful. During the retreat, one of the guys called out myself and Paul Tu'ivai for being overweight. We committed to each other to look after ourselves. It came from a place of care and love, but its never nice to hear it what was said.

What I realized is every good thing that I ever achieved was originally a gift-wrapped problem. Most people don't know how or are unprepared to unwrap the problems, and therefore miss the opportunity to enjoy the gifts of life.

After the retreat twenty of the eighty got covid. I had a lucky escape. If that wasn't enough, one week later, Mighty Paul had a heart attack and died. Life is fragile, and it's so important to live it fully, we don't know when our day is coming. Everytime I go to eat something unhealthy I see his face. I've got to get fit and healthy otherwise I will be joining him in sooner than necessary.

Your environment does not define you, it allows you an opportunity to show the world who you are. Back in the office, we had the best performance of our magazine for five years, the highest magazine revenue for five years, record revenues on ReachTV and London and Singapore are inspired by a trip to Miami for a party of all parties.

You have to set yourself unrealistic targets, you have to find ways to push yourself to think bigger and more creatively. You need to eliminate any small thinking. Stop being scared to take big bites out of the apple of life, and if you want to change the world, look for the great in every person you meet.

55

DECEMBER 2021

DECEMBER DEALS STARTED rolling in on the 1st, and we sold out all our NFL games. According to our TV partners, what we were doing was not possible! Well, welcome to the Ink way of doing things, we do the impossible. My wife says I should train my sales thinking to the competition, but I'm happy keeping the Ink plane going. The new variant arrives in California and the Dow Jones performs a thousand-point swing from over five hundred up to five hundred down. The airline stocks get hammered, I'm gonna start buying soon. We do our first sponsorship deal for PlayersTV in less than a week. This is going to be a fun business too.

I'm negotiating with the NFL to get VVVIP tickets to the Super Bowl – it is going to set us back about half a million dollars. It feels nice to be making brave moves again. On December 7th, I met Steve Clarke for lunch, and he is thinking he's got to buy me lunch, he's not expecting the current me to walk in, happy and positive. When I share that we are back in profit, he breaks down into tears – what a reaction, he was so happy for me. Most people's belief that we should not still be in business. We really should not have survived.

As I am sitting on the plane to Miami en route to Puerto Rico for our holiday party, I realize that it's about to get fun. I have a very exciting business on my hands, and I start to brain-dump ideas about how I can grow this into the juggernaut it deserves to be.

The week of partying begins and I am grateful to all those who supported me and the business rebound. It's quite an emotional time, as we reflect on how far we have come. At about midnight, I let the kids carry on, and they drank the bar dry. I fly to NY in the morning for a catch-up with our investors and partner companies.

NY is freezing, and two days in a boardroom on the sixty-fifth floor of the World Trade Center leaves me exhausted. Gotta get back to Miami for the final Ink Christmas party, where so many have flown in from all over the world. We head to Gulfstream Park for a party and karaoke – I think we might have overdone it on the partying, these kids have no stamina!

I decided to write everyone a personalized handwritten thank you note, to show my appreciation.

One more party for me; after a day of meeting the PlayersTV team, and doing our first sponsorship deal for PlayersTV, we party until the early hours. I have three more meetings in Dallas before I head to Vegas to meet my wife and son for a wind-down to end the year.

I'm in Vegas, playing poker, and something dawns on me; I'm sitting at a one/three-dollar table. The game is the same as the twenty-five/fifty-dollar table, the difference is that you can win hundreds at one, but at the other you can win so much more. Business is the same during this pandemic, I found out that I moved tables. I didn't want to play small anymore. You know why some people do bigger deals? They just ask for them. That's it, nothing more.

I see David Meltzer, Brad Lea and Chris Voss in Vegas and get a chance to show my appreciation for their help during this period. They are all amazed by the story and are genuinely happy for me.

As we come to the end of the year, we as a business started to ask for more. We were not going back to small thinking, small behaviors, and being small-time. The final big deal of the year comes in, and as Christmas Eve rings in, I'm in Mexico. I am starting to switch off. The news headlines suck; Omicron is rife and spreading like wildfire across Europe and the US. For the first time the passenger number surpassed the same date in 2019. The teams compile their letters to the future. We compile these letters every year, it's a forward looking letter looking back at the year, including all the things you want to achieve. It's our form of ordering what we want the year to look like. Mine ends in Bali, having taken my boys to the World Cup final in Qatar.

Everybody needs to go through hell and have something nearly destroy their business to understand who they are and how strong they can be.

This isn't over yet, but my belief is back, and remember, this success is driven by belief.

We live in a transactional world and you can't solve long-term problems with 'now' living. I realize I need to have bigger dreams going forward. I don't just want to get a little better, I want to have a moonshot.

The year ends dancing the night away in Puerto Vallarta. A cigar in hand, sat round the fire pit. I am emotionally so happy. I did what I said I would do and I genuinely cannot wait to get back to work next week.

As we finish the year, this virus is out of control again; despite everyone's best intentions. I think they are starting to realize they cannot control it. I told them that two years ago.

In June this year we had lost in the region of $6.5 million, but by the end of year my mission was to get the business back into profitability. I think we will top $7 million, thanks to a whopping turnaround; as a testament to my team and the business, we transformed. After two years of fighting battle after battle, I finally felt a sense of pride.

With the benefit of hindsight, the failures, challenges and adventures I endured allowed me to narrate this book for you. Please understand I was failing for such a long period; therefore, this book was written by someone who was desperate to get back to winning but ultimately, was a loser and at times a complete failure. It's clear to me, that when you are at your lowest ebb, is when the greatest growth appears. When things look darkest it's just you fumbling for the light switch.

I can tell you the lights are back on and without constant and unbreakable belief none of this would have been possible. While this story might be ending, it's far from over. Please do follow me on social media as I continue my journey, and don't be surprised if my next move is a much bigger one.

56

HOW THE HELL DID
IT FINISH

WHAT TRANSPIRED WAS over ninety weeks of hell. In that time, we lost over two hundred staff members, most of our clients, and most of our ability to make money, but no one seemed to care.

Suppliers didn't seem to care very much either; they wanted to be paid, no matter what. The big tech companies offered no reprise either – Salesforce, Microsoft and Adobe were unhelpful. In the end, Salesforce offered us a small concession after I took a pretty aggressive approach through social media. I spent countless hours questioning the logic of many government officials. Their decision-making, the lack of strategy, and inability to get the world moving again. Everything seemed so illogical, from staying in and going out, to masks and working from home. They all seemed to contradict each other.

While travel and media were bullseye in the middle of this crisis, many companies did well. Many new companies flourished. My son left our business in late 2020 and started a small influencer business in his bedroom. By the end of 2021, he had built up the fastest-growing agency in the UK.

Many podcasters asked me what advice I would give to my twenty-one-year-old self, and here I was able to demonstrate that every day, giving my son my best advice. My son is a chip off the old block, and may his business go from strength to strength. It has also been great to see my playbook played out in a different business. While I was in Mexico, he had his whole team in the Maldives for Christmas. It makes me happy, proud, and also pleased that my system does really work in any industry.

57

FINAL LESSON

I LEARNED SO MUCH about myself, about how resilient I could be, how much strength I had. I read great books during this period which helped me, and my team came through. I have always been a little bit disparaging of myself. I would say, what happens when they figure out, I haven't got a clue what I'm doing? I realized through this time that I was bloody competent and actually held everyone and everything together. That I had nerves of steel and belief not many would have had in the same situation. That I had the trust of many, and some brilliant ideas. I was able to build great friendships. I found out that I was braver than I realized and had muscles I hadn't used before.

I went to lots of places, travel keeps me sane. I was the light at the end of the tunnel for the business. My light stayed on throughout, my energy waned from time to time, but overall, I really was strong and focused. I used to think a lot, I walked a lot and very much relied on my learnings to get me through.

I started a hundred conversations with interesting people. I started to write poems to clear my head. The @themotivationalpoet started in January 2021, and at the end of the year, I published a book with over 380 poems and sent a copy to all our clients.

There's a reason that your car windscreen is bigger than the rear-view mirror – you're heading in that direction, and all the opportunity and risk lies ahead. Any time spent comparing your financial position or results to the previous year is a waste of time. My focus was 100% directed on the weeks and months ahead – we started to measure how much our business has grown from 1st April 2020, rather than how much it shrank from high peaks of 2019.

We had to act with urgency as the cash began to diminish. Acting with urgency is not the same as being short-termist, and certainly not the same as panicking. We had to prepare for a different future and stop comparing today with last year. Although, in some months we actually beat last year, despite a near seventy percent drop in traffic – go figure that one out.

We did manage to make money in 2021, which was a remarkable turnaround. That was only made possible by the lessons we learned in lockdown, and I know if you use some of the lessons in this playbook in good times, your team's results will be nothing short of amazing.

Remember, this is not a book just for difficult times. It's time to think about why the hell you are in business; not why you started, but why you continue to pay yourself less than the average senior executive and work sixty-plus hours a week. Why do you put yourself through challenges and stress? Why do you choose to miss family time, and why are you always distracted? Why do you put others ahead of yourself and get disappointed by the lack of appreciation?

Maybe it's time to burn the bridges and start again. This book will hopefully have given you ideas to change your world – it changed mine and has allowed me to enjoy my life. I live in a place of 'I don't mind what happens, I'll make the best of it, I am fully committed to the task ahead, but totally unattached to what unfolds'. I realized that there was nothing wrong with who I am or what I was achieving. This was a year when some stuff happened and I dealt with it, for the most part, in the best way I could. I could live with whatever the downside was, and pointed everyone in the direction of the upside.

I loved discovering who I am, what I'm really capable of, how much stamina and strength I had, who I could count on, and who let me down badly. I learned that I really was good at what I did, that I had the ability to spot talent, and to nurture that talent in and out of the business. That I was a good networker and built the trust of people who let me into their circles. I found out that the pursuit of anything – happiness, success, wealth or a good reputation – is the problem. They are all in all of us, it's our job to bring them out, if we want to. I realized that happiness came from not searching for happiness.

I want to thank all the people who contributed to this book, to all the people at Ink today, and those that left on good or bad terms during the last two years. I hope none of us need to experience a challenge like this ever again. At least we will be armed and ready for the next one.

Because one thing is for sure, the next problem is just around the corner.

LAST WORDS

IT SEEMS A GOOD TIME to really thank those who stood shoulder to shoulder with me and remained resolute throughout this challenging period: Steve Rowbotham, Gerry Ricketts, Mark Duke, Denise Jaschke, Alyson Rosen, Felix Ramirez, Shalu Ramakrishnan, Lynn Ashlee, Agnelli Bas, Sofian Zainis, Matteo Cappelletti, Christian Fernandez, Annie Alvarez, Brian Stromlund, Louise Burt, Daniella Hernandez, David Brown, Jess Rehki, Billy Vance, Mark Kubatov, Marie Yeo, Aurelia Goetz, Albert Birchwolf, Nadine Merkel and Michael Morris. I really appreciate you all more than you will ever know.

Thanks also to Bob Burg of the *Go Giver* and Michael Bungay Stainer, *the Coaching Habit* for sending inspiring videos to the team.

GOOD BOOKS TO READ

THE ROAD LESS STUPID by Keith J. Cunningham
MAN'S SEARCH FOR MEANING by Viktor E Frankl
GO-GIVER GUIDE TO SELLING by Bob Burg
GREENLIGHTS by Matthew McConaughey
HAPPY SEXY MILLIONAIRE by Steven Bartlett
GETTING NAKED by Patrick Lencioni
48 LAWS OF POWER by Robert Greene

I would love to know what you
thought of Equanimity! You can write
a review with your thoughts at:

AMAZON, GOODREADS and **FACEBOOK**

ABOUT THE AUTHOR

SIMON LESLIE IS joint Chief Executive of Ink, a global travel media company. He is responsible for delivering high performance and helping leave people better than he finds them. He is married with four boys and spends his time between London, Singapore, and Miami.

He has investments in a few start-ups and mentors the owners of these companies. Simon coaches many high performance individuals and all the mantras in this book are his, or kindly borrowed from his many mentors and coaches over the years.

Having built Ink into a $100m+ business, the pandemic ravaged the company and its products. He is currently living his best life while rebuilding the company to be even bigger and more profitable. Follow him on Linkedin for monthly updates.

For more information on this and his other books, *No F in Sales*, *White Belt Thinking*, and *Feel Good* visit *luckyleslie.com* or *follow @themotivationalpoet on Instagram*.

Made in the USA
Columbia, SC
09 November 2022

70709472R00196